# TRUMAN CAPOTE'S SOUTHERN YEARS

# TRUMAN CAPOTE'S SOUTHERN YEARS

*Stories from a Monroeville Cousin*

**Marianne M. Moates**

The University of Alabama Press
Tuscaloosa and London

The University of Alabama Press
Tuscaloosa, Alabama 35487-0380

Paperback printing 2008

Photographs and letters courtesy of Jennings Faulk Carter, with exception of Monroe County Courthouse courtesy of Aaron White Photography; Hatter's Mill, courtesy of Marion Smith; street scenes, courtesy of The Monroe Journal.

Grateful acknowledgment is made to Random House, Inc., for permission to quote from the following copyrighted works of Truman Capote: Other Voices, Other Rooms © 1948; A Tree of Night and Other Stories © 1949; Local Color © 1950; The Grass Harp © 1951; "A Christmas Memory" © 1966; "The Thanksgiving Visitor" © 1967; The Dogs Bark: Public People and Private Places © 1973; and Music for Chameleons © 1980.

∞

The paper on which this book is printed meets the minimum requirements of American National Standard for Information Science—Permanence of Paper for Printed Library Materials, ANSI Z39.48-1984.

Library of Congress Cataloging-in-Publication Data

Moates, Marianne M. (Marianne Merrill)
[Bridge of childhood]
Truman Capote's southern years : stories from a Monroeville cousin / Marianne M. Motes.
p. cm.
Originally published: A bridge of childhood. New York : H. Holt, © 1989
Organized and written from the tape-recorded reminiscences of Jennings Faulk Carter.
Includes Index.
ISBN 978-0-8173-5527-2 (pbk.: alk. paper)
1. Capote, Truman, 1924– —Homes and haunts—Alabama—Monroeville. 2. Capote, Truman, 1924– —Childhood and youth. 3. Authors, American—20th century—Family relationships. 4. Monroeville (Ala.)—Social life and customs. 5. Monroeville (Ala.)—Biography. I. Carter, Jennings Faulk. II Title.
PS3505.A59Z69 1996
813' .54—dc20
[ B]                                                                    95-23384

*To the memory of*
*Sook, Jenny, Callie, and Bud Faulk*
*and their little buddy, Truman Capote.*
*And for Truman's young friends,*
*Nelle and Big Boy.*

# CONTENTS

# ACKNOWLEDGMENTS

These stories were organized and written from the tape-recorded reminiscences of Jennings Faulk Carter, cousin of Truman Capote. In preparing the reminiscences for publication, I felt both proud and grateful for this unique experience: to witness and to share with readers the escapades of the childhood playmates—Jennings Faulk Carter, Truman Capote, and Nelle Harper Lee—growing up in Monroeville, Alabama. Often reminiscences of childhood days are bittersweet, and the experiences related here of the two boy cousins and their neighbor have that quality, while providing insight on their young lives. We can laugh and cry with them.

My gratitude goes to Jennings Faulk Carter for spending many hours preparing tapes of his boyhood experiences with Truman Capote; for searching through musty stacks of family photographs to find the few remaining ones of Capote as a child; for painstakingly researching old family records and documents to prepare the Faulk family genealogy; for patiently reading and critiquing the manuscript and offering suggestions; for taking me on treks through briar-covered old cemeteries and abandoned homesites; and for entrusting me with all the information.

As I worked on the manuscript, sometimes at daybreak, at other times until midnight, my husband, Jim, never complained about the disruption of our normal family routine. Jim and our children joined me in the excitement of watching a new work come to life, and I feel blessed by their attitude.

I don't know what I would have done without the assistance of my dear friend Ruth Beaumont, who, in spite of a heavy writing and teaching schedule of her own, found time to critique each story in its early stages. Her honest appraisal kept the writing on a sound course, and the manuscript is better for her guidance.

Only another artist can understand fully the magnitude of the creative process and the demands upon the one ultimately responsible for producing the work. So I am grateful for the camaraderie of fellow writing friends who offered encouragement on those days when I felt bogged down.

I also wish to thank George D. H. McMillan, Jr., of Birmingham, Alabama, my agent, attorney, and friend, who gave countless hours to the business of the book, and my editor, Peter Bejger, for his help in making the book become a reality.

M. M.

# Truman Capote: A Family Tree

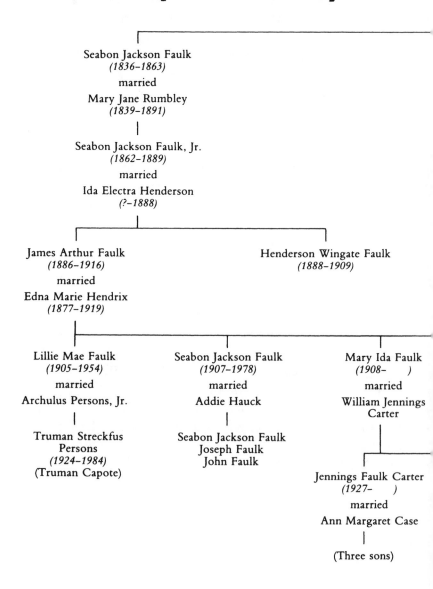

Seabon Jackson Faulk
*(1836–1863)*
married
Mary Jane Rumbley
*(1839–1891)*

Seabon Jackson Faulk, Jr.
*(1862–1889)*
married
Ida Electra Henderson
*(?–1888)*

James Arthur Faulk
*(1886–1916)*
married
Edna Marie Hendrix
*(1877–1919)*

Henderson Wingate Faulk
*(1888–1909)*

Lillie Mae Faulk
*(1905–1954)*
married
Archulus Persons, Jr.

Truman Streckfus
Persons
*(1924–1984)*
(Truman Capote)

Seabon Jackson Faulk
*(1907–1978)*
married
Addie Hauck

Seabon Jackson Faulk
Joseph Faulk
John Faulk

Mary Ida Faulk
*(1908–     )*
married
William Jennings
Carter

Jennings Faulk Carter
*(1927–     )*
married
Ann Margaret Case

(Three sons)

William Jasper Faulk
*(1839–1899)*

married

Samantha Rumbley
*(1842–1913)*

John Byron "Bud" Faulk
*(1869–1934)*

Nanny Rumbley "Sook" Faulk
*(1871–1946)*

Virginia Hurd "Jenny" Faulk
*(1873–1958)*

Caroline Elizabeth "Callie" Faulk
*(1875–1937)*

Richard Howard Faulk
*(1879–1959)*

Mary Denard Faulk
*(1879–1944)*

William Wingate Faulk
*(died in infancy)*

Edna Marie Faulk
*(1911–    )*

married

James E. Rudisell

James M. Rudisell

George Faulk
*(1913–1914)*

A. Lucille Faulk
*(1915–    )*

married

James G. Ingram

Cecelia Melissa Ingram

John Byron Carter
*(1936–    )*

married

Shirley Anne
Coleman

(One daughter;
four sons)

*Bud, Sook, Jenny, and Callie raised James Arthur Faulk; J. A. Faulk's children, including Lillie Mae; and her son, Truman, from 1928 to 1934.

# TRUMAN CAPOTE'S SOUTHERN YEARS

# PROLOGUE

*T*his book began in April 1961, when I moved to Monroeville, Alabama (population about 3,500 back then), with my husband, Jim, and our baby son, Ben. Jim had recently finished a stint as an army pilot at Fort Rucker, Alabama. We were glad to have his military obligation over with and be "settling down" to raise a family just sixty miles west of Andalusia, where we both had grown up. Jim had a job as an engineer in a garment manufacturing plant still referred to by the locals as "the silk mill."

We moved into the neighborhood where Truman Capote and Nelle Harper Lee, Monroeville's most famous citizens, had grown up. (To her friends and family in Monroeville, Harper Lee is known as Nelle.) Our wood-frame house, with its high ceilings and big, open rooms, was vintage 1930s. Living there was almost like being back home. Monroeville was a small town with tree-lined sidewalks, a downtown square, and friendly people who lived in houses with big front porches.

When I arrived in Monroeville that spring, the town was dizzy with excitement over Nelle Harper Lee's book, *To Kill a Mockingbird,* winner of a Pulitzer Prize. There were coffees and socials for Nelle, some of which I happily attended, having been invited by new acquaintances. It was an exciting time, but one filled with tense, whispered gossip as well. Almost all those who had known Nelle in the 1930s through the fifties thought they saw themselves in her book. Others declared aloud, "Nelle's childhood friend, Truman Capote— the famous writer—wrote her book." Gossip had it that one family was threatening to sue because the character Boo Radley was too much like one of their own family members. When Nelle had had enough, she reminded people that her book was fiction, zipped her lips shut, and caught the next plane back to New York.

Nevertheless, I was intrigued by all the brouhaha, and I used those first few months to explore the terrain. The grammar school was only two blocks away. With Ben in his stroller, I walked by there almost every day, fascinated by the knowledge that one of the big oak trees on the school grounds was the tree where Boo Radley had hidden trinkets for Scout and Jem in *To Kill a Mockingbird.* I often walked two blocks beyond the school grounds to the rambling white frame house of the Faulks on South Alabama Avenue, where Truman Capote spent much of his youth. A thick rock fence made of limestone from a nearby creek practically walled in the yard. I pictured a scene straight from "A Christmas Memory," with the little boy Truman and his beloved Sook in the backyard gathering pecans for their fruitcake project each Thanksgiving. And I could almost hear the childhood voices of Truman and his next-door neighbor, Nelle Harper Lee, playing in the yard.

About four blocks from my house, in the center of town, stood the tired red-brick courthouse, supposedly where Atticus Finch defended a wronged black man in Nelle's novel. Old men gathered under the spreading oak trees and played checkers for hours at a time. Traffic moved lazily around the square, and shoppers strolled in and out of businesses. Although it was 1961, from the look of things, it could just as easily have been 1931.

Even though I lived in Monroeville for eight years, I could not have written this particular book without information from Jennings Faulk Carter, Truman Capote's cousin. The two boys grew up together. This information came over the next several years as Jim and I became close friends with members of the Carter family. My association with them came about quite by accident.

In December 1961, Jim went on a deer hunt in Monroe County and met Jennings Faulk Carter, a crop duster who flew an aged yellow Steerman, a biplane with an open cockpit. He even did his own mechanical work on the plane to keep it airborne. The two men took an immediate liking to each other, as they had flying and hunting interests to share. Jennings Faulk invited us to his home in the small community of Mexia, west of Monroeville, to meet his wife, Ann, and their two young sons, Steven and Frank. I was very pregnant at the time with my second son, Mike, and relished the idea of making new friends. Our first meeting was an immediate success, and we began a friendship that is now more than twenty-five years old.

In the months that followed I spent many pleasant hours with Ann and Jennings Faulk in their country house. In the summer Ann and I snapped beans and shelled peas from her garden, drank coffee, and watched our children play beneath the huge chestnut tree in her backyard. I marveled at the Carters' life-style. There was a grass landing strip beside the house, gasoline tanks and a pump, and a storage area for the chemicals used in the spraying and dusting operation. From early spring to late autumn, Jennings Faulk flew from daylight until dark. In the Deep South, that's from about four-thirty in the morning until nearly nine at night. When Ann heard him buzzing in to refuel, she'd hurry out the screen door with messages from the farmers who had called to have their soybeans and cotton sprayed or dusted with poison.

"Old man Jones'll be out beside the field waving a white flag when you fly over," she said. "And when you go to the Rays' place, they've got it marked on one end by a red tractor; on the other are three stakes with yellow flags." And through some special understanding of the people and times, Jennings Faulk knew which field, where, and how much of it to spray or dust. After filling the tanks, he buckled on his leather helmet and goggles, strapped himself in, and waited for Ann to give the giant propeller a spin. As the wooden prop spun around with a roar, Ann jumped back in time to keep from being slashed to death.

Both Jennings Faulk and Ann were tall, lanky, sun-scorched people who were nearly worked to death in the summer. But we always managed to do some things together that were fun. On Sunday afternoons we piled the kids into an old pickup truck and drove to the Alabama beaches to play for a day. Or we went down to Little River, where still, clear pools reflected big bass swimming lazily along. We poked around old cemeteries at Claiborne, looked for Indian and Civil War relics for the Carters' collections, told Indian legends about Red Eagle, who once lived in that area, went target shooting with our pistols, picknicked, swam, took flying trips to New Orleans in their four-seater plane, and cooked steaks and venison in the backyard. Sometimes Jennings Faulk's younger brother, John Byron, his wife, Shirley, and their four children (a girl and three boys) were along. John Byron would bring out the guitar, pick a tune, and we'd sing and laugh and read poetry.

On winter days, when the Carters had more leisure, we'd talk for hours about politics, the war in Vietnam, religion, liberals who were taking over the country, the civil rights movement and what it would mean to our little isolated world if and when integration came, rockets shooting off into space, too much/too little rain and what an abundance/lack of it meant to the Carters' agricultural spraying business, the old farmer who always paid Ann six hundred dollars in cash that had been wadded in his old coveralls, the new Monroe County airport, Nelle's success with *To Kill a Mockingbird,* and Jennings Faulk's "weird little cousin," Truman Capote, who occasionally left his fame and glittery life behind and visited them in Monroeville.

Sometimes, over a bourbon and water, Jennings Faulk told wonderful stories of the times he, Truman, and Nelle Harper Lee had enjoyed as children. Jennings Faulk had spent many hours at Jenny Faulk's house, where Truman lived as a child. The two first cousins were as close as brothers. Nelle, their next-door neighbor, was their pal, confidante, and, at times, sparring partner. The three conspired in Nelle's tree house to play pranks; they made popguns, swam in the creek, staged carnivals, and told tales with Sook. It is stories about these times, drawn from real-life incidents, that form the basis of this book.

Having known the Faulk family for more than twenty-five years, and known Truman through them, I realized that even though biographies had been written about Truman's life, the whole story had not been told. Very little has been written about the early life of Truman Streckfus Persons— Truman Capote. Nelle Lee models the peculiar little boy, Dill, after Truman, in *To Kill a Mockingbird*. But since her novel is fiction, doubt remains as to how close the character really is to Truman. So we turn to Truman for answers. He gives us glimpses of himself in several of his works: *Other Voices, Other Rooms; The Grass Harp;* "The Thanksgiving Visitor"; "A Christmas Memory"; and "One Christmas." Except for these mostly fictional works and a few comments in interviews, however, that's all we know about the little boy who was to grow up and become Truman Capote, writer.

Fortunately, Jennings Faulk Carter has shared another view. Truman was "different" from the very beginning. He had a marvelous gift with words, and so he began to write. First, the truth; then the truth enlarged with fantasy. He scribbled notations in a small notebook he carried all the time. "Words to describe how a tree looked draped across a creek, a male and female dog tied together in mating, how the sunlight looked on a pile of leaves," says Jennings Faulk Carter. "He was always writing down descriptions of things. He trained with a pencil and paper in the same way that a musician works with notes, or an artist with colors."

Another thing we know about Truman Capote is that he was very close to his Monroeville family. He may claim to have been lonely and misunderstood, but he was very much cared for by his Faulk relatives, at least as long as he was a child. As he grew into manhood, he strayed from their Southern traditional family values, and this was hard for family members to accept. He maintained a close relationship with his aunt, Mary Ida Carter, throughout his life. "Home" to him was the comfortable Carter farmhouse on Drewry Road, about two miles from Monroeville.

The stories in this book are intended to shed light on what life was like in Truman's boyhood home. Serious students of Capote will no doubt seek to interpret the tales. That is not for me to do. I wish only to report information too valuable for history to overlook. And this is why I also point out what life was like in the Carter household when we lived in Monroeville: it may lead us to a deeper understanding of Capote.

Sometime during the early years of my relationship with the Carters, Jennings Faulk and Ann moved from Mexia, west of Monroeville, across town to Drewry Road. They bought property near Jennings Faulk's parents' farm and near his brother, John Byron Carter, who was living in the Ryland house, although the Rylands had long since moved away. The new brick house was one story, with three bedrooms, a formal living-dining room for their Victorian furniture, and a comfortable den-kitchen combination, where we spent most of our time together. The new property had a bigger area for a landing strip and hangar and some pasture for cows.

Each fall, Jennings Faulk took his cattle to the slaughterhouse. He'd pick out a steer and have it butchered for the freezer at home. When our families gathered for a meal, Ann and I made a production of dinner, because that's the way things were done back in those days. Ann bought milk from an old woman who lived not far from her on a dirt road. It was wonderful milk in tall, round, scalded jugs. Ann skimmed off the cream, whipped it with sugar, and piled it high on hot, spicy pear pies. Once we spent the morning picking clumps of dark red cherries from a fence of wild cherry trees by her house. We made wine using an old family recipe belonging to her mother-in-law, Mary Ida Carter. As we lived in a "dry" county, we often made wine. From time to time we even bought good-quality "shinny," or bootleg whiskey, made palatable by mixing it with sweetened grapefruit juice, then downed quickly while we held our noses. If we wanted bourbon we had to drive fifty miles across the county line to Brewton.

Jennings Faulk's parents, Mary Ida and Jennings, lived close by. The elder Jennings was a tall, tanned man who was always smiling. Mary Ida was almost as high as his shoulders. A feisty little woman, she made up in opinions and dogma what she lacked in size. The elder Carters often stopped by for coffee and chitchat when we were visiting their son's house. In one conversation, out of earshot of Mary Ida, Jennings asked, "How's Nellie?"

I was a little surprised. "My mother-in-law? She's fine. How do you know her?"

He grinned. "Years ago, when I was a boy living in Troy, I'd ride my horse over to visit some of my family near Andalusia. I used to date a pretty girl there by the name of Nellie Gantt."

"Jim's mother?"

"We go back a long way."

I couldn't help thinking what a small world we lived in, when Mary Ida said, in a voice loud enough to grab everyone's attention, "Truman's coming to see me one day soon." As though she weren't sure Jim and I would know what she meant, she explained, "He's not a Carter, you know. I mean he is, and he isn't. He's my sister's boy, but has his stepdaddy's name—Capote. I think I'll give a little party for him and Nelle. Lots of their friends, teachers, and the family'll want to see them. Truman's off on some scheme. This time he's taking Nelle with him," she said, waving her hand up toward heaven. "Never know what he'll write next. He told me he was going to write about some hooligans who murdered a whole family out in Kansas. Can't imagine why he'd want to write about that! Can you?"

*What a bone-chilling subject,* I thought. "No, I can't imagine why he'd want to."

"He writes all kinds of things," said Jennings. "I think my favorite was 'A Christmas Memory' because we all loved Sook so much."

Mary Ida jumped back into the conversation. "Well, if *he* loved her like he carried on, why in the world did he paint the pore woman as some know-nothing. Sook wadn't like that at all. She might have been a little slow, but she wadn't nothing like Truman made her out to be. We weren't pore! Why, he had the two of them stealing pecans! We didn't have to steal pecans. We had all the pecans we wanted. Christmas presents, too. They didn't have to hide out and make kites. I don't know why Truman said all those things."

"He likes a good story, Mother," offered Jennings Faulk. "He knows what will sell."

"Well, he ought to try selling the truth. The truth don't hurt nobody."

"Yeah, but who'd want to read it?" Jennings Faulk said.

Mary Ida was tired of talking about that, so she invited Jim and me to her party.

And at that moment, I had some idea of why Truman would want to come home. Home was a comfortable old farmhouse presided over by his aunt and uncle, Mary Ida and Jennings Carter. He had his own room where he liked to sink down in a soft bed covered with hand-made quilts and look out his window and see Mary Ida's daylily garden filled with orange and yellow trumpets glorying in their one day to bloom. The kitchen table was piled high with rolled biscuits, dripping in butter and molasses, sitting next to platters of smothered chicken and rice, green beans picked fresh from the garden, and banana pudding with mounds of fluffy white meringue. Home was deep woods and dirt roads whose overgrown ditches smelled of sweet honeysuckle perfume; the cows lowing on rolling green pastures along Drewry Road; the smell of cow dung; and the sight of new calves.

When he drove through town he'd notice a few changes. More traffic. More noise. The movie house was now open on weeknights. Some new churches were going up. The old Faulk home near the courthouse square was still there, needing a coat of paint. The Lee house, whose backyard had joined the Faulk house, was gone now, replaced by an ice-cream store. Some of the favorite play haunts—hedges, trees, and garages—were gone. But the big schoolyard and the old rock fence would beckon like friends, saying, "Welcome back to the South and the family that raised you."

Yes, Truman Capote was coming home, back to the mothering South, before going somewhere in Kansas to research and write about some murderers.

This was one party I wasn't going to miss.

*I*'ll never forget that warm Sunday afternoon of the tea party. It was April 1963. Jim and I drove up the winding dirt road to the Carter farmhouse, parked on the grass, and walked to the front door. The house was decorated from top to bottom with orange and yellow lilies from Mary Ida's garden. Pink and white roses floated in silver trays. The guests filtered in; men wore suits and starched shirts that stuck to their backs on this hot afternoon. The ladies wilted in filmy summer dresses with lace collars. It was a time of renewal, of saying "Hello" and "How are you?" to Nelle, the hometown girl who'd made it big in New York, and her lifetime friend, Truman Capote. After all, the Pulitzer Prize was Nelle's, and a movie about her book had just been released. People fussed around her, holding copies of the book for her autograph.

Not so with Truman. A short, stocky man only five feet three inches tall, Truman had a round face, a slight bald spot at the back of his head, piercing blue eyes looking out from behind horn-rimmed glasses, and a voice that would stop you cold in your tracks before you got used to the pitch and whine. He wore a white shirt without a coat or tie, dark trousers, and dark, wing-tipped shoes. Oh, everybody was polite to him, but nobody knew what to make of him. He had been big on the New York scene for fifteen years. Critics had acclaimed his work, but it had been five years since the success of *Breakfast at Tiffany's,* and this was "old" success compared to Nelle's current hit.

But rather than play the part of "bastard at the family reunion," he adopted a new role: that of a darling. He reveled in the fact that he could grab attention, just by being different. His size alone was an oddity, for most everyone at the party except his aunt, Mary Ida, and her younger son, John Byron, towered over him. Mary Ida and John Byron were nearer Truman's height and build—short and squatty. Jennings and Jennings Faulk were over six feet tall.

Truman held a glass cup of fruit punch (heaven forbid that anybody would openly serve liquor in a dry county on Sunday afternoon!), sipped it holding his little pinky finger curled up, then smacked his lips as if to get every drop. He greeted the guests with a "Hellloooo" in a voice that ran the scales from top to bottom, then kissed the ladies' hands. "It's so goooood to see you." Nobody seemed to know what to say to him or how to talk to him. But I had noticed him watching me, so I decided to try, not knowing whether to call him Truman or Mr. Capote. I decided on Truman.

"Oh, you're Big Boy [he'd called Jennings Faulk "Big Boy" since the two were children] and Ann's friend," he said. "You must be all right."

I was puzzled. "All right?"

"Well, Big Boy doesn't have many friends, so if you're his friend, then you're all right."

"Oh," I said rather timidly. "I guess this means I passed the test."

He threw back his head and laughed. "So what do you do here in Monroeville? Gad! That anybody had to live here!"

"I like it. It's a good place to raise a family."

"You have a family? Tell me about them."

"I have two young sons," I said, and watched him nearly choke on the punch and tea cake. "My husband works for the mill. We hunt and fish." I could tell by the ho-hum look on his face that my description of these plebeian activities was getting this conversation nowhere. Then I decided to sneak in a daring thought. "I like to write."

"Oh, another writer! What do you write?"

"Well, I want to write a novel. Maybe something about the Civil War, someday."

"Do you want to know how to find really good material? The kind *no*body on earth has but you? Just go to a family Sunday dinner and *listen*. By the time the meal is over and everybody has had his say at the table, you'll be brimming over with stories."

I smiled.

"Write about something you know," he said. Then he quickly put down the punch cup as if just remembering something important, grabbed my hand, and rushed me toward the door. "Come see my new car!" he said. When we passed Jennings Faulk and Jim talking on the porch, he motioned for them to follow us down the front steps and into the yard, where he pulled the hood latch on his shiny new Jaguar. "Oh, look," he began, entwining his fingers in front of him, "see this lovely engine." Then he motioned for us to come around to the trunk of the car. He slipped the key in the lock and the trunk top sprung open. There sat a case of black-label Jack Daniel's whiskey. "Now when the rest of these people have gone home, *we're* going to have a party," he said, grinning with delight.

As the party guests faded away one by one, dusk settled over the gently sloping pastures at Drewry. Truman went out to the car and brought in two bottles of his favorite whiskey, hot from being cooped up inside the trunk. "Okay, darling Mary Ida, what kind of mixer do you have for these good people?"

Jennings Faulk answered before Mary Ida could get a word in. "Mixer! Why, don't dare pollute that good stuff with mixer! Just give us a little ice and some water, Mother."

Mary Ida filled a cut-glass pitcher and the ice bucket and set out several short glasses. Truman twirled the top off the bottle and poured drinks for his aunt and uncle, Ann and Jennings Faulk; John Byron and his wife, Shirley; and Jim and me. The warm liquid slid down our throats. We laughed, told dirty jokes, and talked until the moon was high. I was fascinated by all that Truman had to say.

"Yes, I'm researching this grisly murder of an entire family out in Kansas. I'm interviewing the murderers, taking notes furiously, and will write an account of the event," he said with assurance. "It will be a new kind of writing. I'm calling it a *nonfiction novel.* May even find me a little place in the country around here and make a writer's hideaway so I can work."

As the hour grew late, I knew I had to go back home to my little boys. It was time to say good-bye. We all hugged and wished one another well. By this time I'd taken off my heels, which had added three inches to my five-foot-nine-inch height. Standing in my stocking feet, I still towered over Truman. We hugged good-bye. "Good luck with your project," he said, giving me a wink. "And good luck with yours," I replied.

I kept up with Truman indirectly through the Carters after that. About two years later, early one December evening, a Saturday night, we were at the Carters' house, children and all, getting ready to eat dinner. It was a sweater-and-wool-slacks night with the wind howling through the chimney. A stack of Christmas presents in bright red and green wrapping stood in the corner waiting for the tree the family would go out and chop down the next afternoon. Ann had built a roaring fire in the den fireplace, and we had put on a stack of Herb Alpert records. It was such a bitter night we opted to cook steaks inside rather than fight icy air over charcoal flames outside. I chopped lettuce for a tossed salad as Ann brought out a pan full of buttery yeast rolls cooked in a black skillet. As we sat down to eat, the phone rang. It was Truman, calling from New York.

Jennings Faulk answered the phone. "Well, hello, Truman. I'll wish you an early Merry Christmas."

"I want you and Ann to spend Christmas with me in Switzerland this year," Truman said.

Jennings Faulk spoke rather slowly. "Well, it surely sounds good, Truman, and we'd like to, but I don't see how we could get over there."

"Just hop on a plane. Bring the boys if you want to. They'd love the skiing and all the snow."

"I'm sure they would, Truman. I'll talk it over with Ann, but don't count on it. Thanks for thinking of us, though."

He hung up the phone and smiled. "That would be quite a trip," he said.

"And quite expensive," Ann added, dark eyes dancing about. There was something in her voice that led us to think *this* family wasn't about to purchase five round-trip tickets to Switzerland. It would be five tickets because Ann and Jennings Faulk had a new son, as did Jim and I.

Another year rolled around, and *In Cold Blood* was published. Almost overnight Truman Capote became a forty-two-year-old millionaire, world-acclaimed author, and one of the most fashionable of the jet-setters. Although more and more out of touch with his Monroeville family, he did call from time to time and sent his aunt postcards and letters that began, "Darling Mary Ida."

In the fall of 1966, when he was planning his Black and White Ball for the elite of two continents, Truman called Jennings Faulk. "I have made all the arrangements. You, Ann, Mary Ida, and Jennings please attend and meet my friends. Most important, I want them to meet you." Again, Truman was put off.

It was an especially pretty time of the year in Monroeville. The oaks, hickories, and dogwood trees were awash with orange, brown, and yellow. Some days the temperatures zoomed up near ninety. I visited Ann one October afternoon, and as we sat outside on the patio and watched the children romp and play, we discussed whether or not they should go to the party.

"You must go," I urged. "How can you *not* go?" I should have known how easy it would be for them not to go. Truman was different. He'd *always* been different. It wasn't enough that he had written strange fiction about bizarre lifestyles, but the family's suspicions were found to be true: he was *living* the bizarre life-style. In his family's eyes and in the eyes of many people in Monroeville, he acted like a kook. He *was* a kook. He wasn't, in his own words, "a saint yet"; he was an eccentric character who drank too much. That was a bitter pill for the family to swallow. This might have been the permissive and promiscuous sixties, but in Monroeville, there was no escaping traditional values. And the Carters had their pride. They did not want to be preened and paraded before Truman's elite friends at some expensive bash. Jennings Faulk had seen Truman use people all his life. It wouldn't be any different this time.

It would be another year before Truman called again. This time he insisted the family join him in Montgomery for the filming of "The Thanksgiving Visitor." The family loaded up in cars and joined him there for several reasons: proximity; it was easy to get to Montgomery; not much was expected; and no fancy clothes or extraordinary effort was involved in spending a day on a movie set. Then there was their adoration of Sook, the heroine of the story. Truman and Jennings Faulk had enjoyed the same relation to Sook. She had loved them equally, cared for them as little boys, and even in death she had their total devotion. Then there was the story itself. It was a family tale about something that might have been. "Only Truman can't stick to the truth," said Mary Ida. But that was Truman. He took nuggets of truth, gave them a new twist, and made them bigger than life.

There is no doubt that the 1960s belonged to Truman Capote. Two weeks after the publication of *In Cold Blood,* the book was on the best-seller list. He reportedly earned two million dollars for the literary triumph. His works *In Cold Blood,* "A Christmas Memory," and "The Thanksgiving Visitor" were adapted for the screen. His fame and personal fortune rose to an all-time high, and he was the darling of the talk-show circuit. He rubbed elbows with celebrities, politicians, movie stars, the wealthy of all different backgrounds. But in the early 1970s something happened.

He lost weight, suffered bouts of depression, and became a victim of alcoholism, a disease that had afflicted several family members on his mother's side, including his cousin Bud, who helped raise him; his Uncle Howard, who was his mother's brother; and his great-grandfather—Bud's father—William Jasper Faulk.

By the mid-1970s Truman was well on the way toward self-destruction. He was arrested for drunken driving; walked incoherently off the stage before 1,200 guests at Towson State University in Baltimore; and underwent alcoholism treatment several times. Gone was the firm, tanned, youthful face, the sometimes giddy voice. His speech was slurred. Puffy, swollen eyes stared into space when he said he wasn't only an alcoholic, but was also one who was doubly addicted, to alcohol and to tranquilizers. He could go weeks or months, try every kind of therapy, but in the end, he said he would drink again. "I don't know why. No analyst, no therapist, psychiatrist, nobody, has ever been able to figure out why to my satisfaction."

The last decade of Truman Capote's life was, in many ways, a living hell. After the booze and pills, a slander suit involving his friend Gore Vidal, and his failure to finish *Answered Prayers* and to keep old friends or make new ones, he had but one final act to play. A few months before he died, he tried to visit Monroeville one last time. He wanted to get back to Aunt Mary Ida, to home. *She'll fluff the feather pillows, cook peas and fresh okra, cut daylilies for the glass pitcher, and heat the buttery biscuits,* he thought. But time and addictions had taken their toll. He never returned to Monroeville.

After Truman died, I began putting the past quarter of a century in perspective, combining it with what I knew about his relationship with his Carter relatives. I realized that the Truman Capote puzzle was only partially complete. A full understanding of the man and his work was centered in his childhood—those precious formative years that bend the twig. I also knew the person who held the missing pieces of the puzzle: Jennings Faulk Carter.

Many years ago Truman said, "Past certain ages or certain wisdoms it is very difficult to look with wonder; it is best done when one is a child; after that, and if you are lucky, you will find a bridge of childhood and walk across it."

Jennings Faulk Carter gave us that bridge of childhood.

—Marianne Merrill Moates

# INTRODUCTION

*When God hands you a gift, he also hands you a whip*
*intended for self-flagellation.*

"Truman Capote," *Vogue*, December 1979

$T$he little town of Monroeville, Alabama (population around 7,500), is known as the "hub." It's a hub because in any direction you must drive for two hours to reach a town of any size. Selma to the north. Montgomery to the northeast. Pensacola to the southeast. Mobile to the southwest. The town sits on red clay hills topped with tall pines and tangled underbrush, still very much like it did when four-year-old Truman Capote moved there in 1928.

His mother, Lillie Mae Faulk Persons, brought him home to Monroeville and abandoned him to the care of some older relatives, all eccentric in their own way. These relatives, the rural atmosphere, and isolation left indelible marks on Truman, however, for he used them all in much of his writing: "A Christmas Memory," "The Thanksgiving Visitor," and "Guests." Monroeville was the setting for *The Grass Harp*, and was Noon City in his first novel, *Other Voices, Other Rooms*. He even began the latter book with "[the] traveller must make his way by the best means he can." Since Truman often came to Monroeville via car over bumpy roads, frequently passing farmers rattling into town in their big old mule-drawn wagons, or on trains that rumbled and clanked through in the night, he knew how difficult it was to get to the scruffy little town.

Although much is known about Truman after he left Monroeville and moved permanently to New York in the early 1940s, very little is known about his childhood years in pre-Depression times, during the Depression, and immediately following. In the rural South in those years, women were still having babies in their homes. Neighbors lived close together. If somebody shouted in the street, people poked their heads out to see what the commotion was all about. Everybody had a turnip patch, chicken coop, hogs, and mules in his backyard. People hung out their wash to flap on the line and thought nothing of it.

Most everybody in town had a colored woman (blacks were referred to as "coloreds" back then) to cook and wash. She walked from Clausell, "the quarters," about a mile west of town. She was a highly prized member of the family, and no one would have dared try to hire her away. Colored men mowed the white folks' yards with push mowers, or kept weeds down with sling blades. They cleaned wood floors with corn-shuck mops, swept the walkways with dogwood brush brooms, and shined windows with ammonia-soaked newspapers. Most everybody in town had electricity, running water in their kitchen sinks, and indoor plumbing. A few houses had telephones. Callers got the other party on the line by calling the operator.

The courthouse was the central attraction in town. The two-story red brick structure stood like a tattered fortress in the middle of the square. A silver cupola, perched on top of the building, held four large clocks that tick-tocked when they wanted to. Old men gathered on the lawn to talk, play checkers, and spit tobacco juice. A horse-hitching rail stood beneath a row of broad-topped oak trees that hung over the streets. None of the streets around the square or in town were paved. They were either red mud or coppery dust, depending on the weather.

In the streets was a strange mixture of horse-drawn wagons, people afoot, and a few automobiles dodging about. Men and women walked to town in the morning, listened for the noon sawmill whistle to tell them to go home for their main meal, then walked back to town for the afternoon's business. In some ways it was a typical little town with a grocery that would deliver, a drugstore with a soda fountain, a livery where farmers could park their horses and wagons, a bank, a furniture store, an ice house, a cotton warehouse, a mercantile store, and some churches—all within a stone's throw of one another. Everybody knew everybody else—and everybody else's business.

Cotton and lumber were the big industries. The gin was just two blocks from town. Wagons piled high with cotton came from miles around to get the cotton ginned, graded, baled, sold, and stored. At ginning time in late summer and early fall, the air was thick with white cotton fluff. People were moving into Monroeville in the late 1920s and needed lumber for new houses, so the sawmill stayed busy.

Truman Capote's Faulk ancestors already had a firm toehold in Monroe County when he came to live there. They ran farms on the outskirts of town without electricity or running water. They were hard-working, pride-filled people who came to Monroeville right after the War of 1812. Family stories have it that royal French ancestors shaped the hands that gripped the plow. Maybe so. Nobody has been able to prove it. William C. Faulk, born in 1819, is of the line of Faulks that leads to Truman on his mother's side. One of William's sons was Seabon Jackson Faulk, born in 1836. With Seabon, a run of hard luck and tragedy entered the family, culminating in the death of Truman Capote.

When the War Between the States began, Seabon left his wife and infant son, Seabon Jr., in Monroeville and went off with his brother, William, to fight for the Southern cause. Seabon didn't make it back; he was killed in the Battle of Atlanta. William scraped by and limped home to the farm on a leg that never healed. He and his wife, Samantha, took in Seabon's wife and baby son, Seabon Jackson, Jr.

While they were raising their nephew, Seabon Jr., in those hard Reconstruction times, they had their own family to feed—John Byron (Bud), Nanny Rumbley (Sook), Virginia Hurd (Jenny), Caroline Elizabeth (Callie), Howard, and Mary. "Home" was a partly log house with two big rooms and a dogtrot down the middle, and enough red dirt to grow a few bales of cotton and some corn. They had lost most of their land to taxes, but Samantha vowed to regain it. Pride and determination kept her struggling against foreclosure.

While William rocked on the front porch, cussed Yankees, and drank laudanum and alcohol for his leg ailment, Samantha went to work in the fields and tried to raise enough food to keep the family from starving. In addition to the cotton and corn, they raised a few cows, pigs, and some vegetables. Taking the children with her, she stuffed moist leaves under their bonnets to keep them from having a heat stroke, and they all worked until they were about to drop in their tracks.

In the Faulk family, the struggle for survival was even harder than for most, because patriarchs were few. Most of the men either died early or suffered from alcohol or drug addictions. Thus the women became the ones to hold the family together. First, it was Samantha. Then her daughter, Jenny Faulk. Jenny is the one who would take in baby Truman and raise him.

Seabon Jr., meanwhile, married when he was seventeen. He and his wife had two sons, Arthur and Wingate. Arthur was to be Truman's grandfather. Seabon's wife died in childbirth when Wingate was born, so Seabon took his young sons and moved to Laurel, Mississippi, and went to work for a turpentine company. He soon contracted TB and died, leaving Arthur, age four, and Wingate, age two, in the piney woods with some ruffians he had worked with.

When Samantha got word that Seabon was dead, she sent her son Bud to Mississippi to get the little boys and bring them back to her. Here is the second generation of orphans that were raised by the same women in the William Jasper Faulk household.

Family stories have it that Arthur was probably a hellion from day one. Some have wondered if he was an outlaw; others say he was shrewd. As a youth, he got himself slammed in the Monroe County jail for stealing an ox. He ran a livery, bought property, and always seemed to have plenty of money during hard times. At age seventeen he began delivering mail along a route linking Monroeville to Mexia and Flomaton. He "overnighted" at the home of Preacher Hendrix in Mexia. The preacher's eldest daughter, Edna Marie, and Arthur eloped to Brewton, about sixty miles away, in 1904. She was twenty-seven, and he was eighteen.

In January 1905, their first child, Lillie Mae, was born. She was to be Truman's mother. Arthur and Edna Marie's other surviving children were Mary Ida, Marie, Seabon, and Lucille. When Lillie Mae was ten, Arthur, age twenty-nine, became ill with TB. A doctor advised him that he was very contagious and that his children could get the disease, so he had a tent erected in his backyard. He lived there for several weeks before he died.

Three years after Arthur Faulk died, his widow, Edna Marie, got sick and went to the hospital in Selma. Several days later Jenny Faulk took the children to the hospital to see their mother and accompany her home. But tragedy seemed to have a never-ending grip on the Faulk children: Edna Marie hemorrhaged and died in the hospital room while Jenny and the children all stood helplessly looking on.

Jenny, meanwhile, had moved to Monroeville and opened a millinery shop. Her business prospered and soon she had enough money to buy two lots. She built a large mercantile store on one lot and a house in town for Bud, Sook, and Callie on the other. Howard and Mary did not move with them because Howard was grown and had moved out, and Mary was married.

After Edna Marie died, Jenny took the children back home with her to the new house on South Alabama Avenue. She gave baby Lucille to Howard and his wife, who were childless. Arthur Faulk's children thus became the third generation of orphans to be raised in the same house with Jenny.

Jenny took control over Arthur's sizable estate. He had left over eight thousand dollars in cash, a livery business, a home and 360 acres, plus a gasoline and oil franchise—a fortune in those days.

Lillie Mae, Truman's mother, was fourteen when she moved in with Jenny, and was never happy at her house. Jenny was a harsh woman who ruled with an iron hand, and Lillie Mae was a tempestuous, angry young woman who needed love and attention. She had lost both her parents and her home. Shouting matches were common between Jenny and Lillie Mae. Jenny tried to cool things between them by sending Lillie Mae away to school, first to a finishing school in Brewton, then to Troy State Teachers' College, but Lillie Mae could not adjust. She wasn't happy in either place, so she returned home to Monroeville to decide her next move.

When Arch Persons roared into Monroeville in his chauffeur-driven Packard touring car, both Lillie Mae and Jenny could see the end in sight for their misery. Lillie Mae saw dollar signs dancing around this "blue-blood" attorney from a prominent Alabama family. The fact that he was a schemer who never practiced law a day in his life was a point to be reckoned with later. Arch and Lillie Mae charmed each other. Arch was captivated by Lillie Mae's striking brunette beauty; she was elated at the idea of marrying money and social position. They wed in a big ceremony at Jenny's house in 1923. Lillie Mae was eighteen years old.

After the wedding, Lillie Mae and Arch moved into the Monteleone Hotel in New Orleans, and for a time, they lived in a grand style. The heart of the city, with its busy French Quarter filled with shops, restaurants, and people, was exciting to a country girl. But Arch's job—traveling between New Orleans and St. Louis with Streckfus Steamship Company—took him away on the boat for weeks at a time, and Lillie Mae spent too much time alone. To compound her problems, she soon learned she was pregnant. She found herself spending more and more time back in Monroeville in the very environment she had sought to escape.

She did not come home to a loving family accepting of their grown child's marital difficulties. Now that she was an adult, they held her at arm's length—a family characteristic that had run through several generations and would also be their attitude toward Truman. Jenny gave Lillie Mae food and a roof over her head, but there was no love, warmth, or family support during this difficult time. The family didn't want her back in the fold. Lillie Mae appealed to her brother, Seabon, for help, but he was a youth and was unable to support her. Unhappily she retreated to New Orleans in late summer to await her child's birth. During the weeks that followed she felt trapped and very much alone at just nineteen years old.

And so it was into this family of "noble blue bloods" that Truman Capote was born Truman Streckfus Persons in Touro Infirmary in New Orleans on September 30, 1924. Five generations of Faulks had taken their first breaths in the pine- and oak-filled woods of Monroe County, Alabama, but baby Truman awoke to a new destiny: he would never hitch a mule, plow to the end of a long, hot row, or chop cotton. His would be a new type of struggle. His crucible would be writing—"the merciless master," he would say of his work. He would want family, love, and a secure environment, but he wanted them on his terms. When he broke with traditional family values, the family turned their backs on him the way they turned their backs on his mother. Even his intellectual genius could not help him find a way to return to the fold.

Although Lillie Mae was strong in some ways, she knew nothing about nurturing a little baby. She did not know *how* to be a mother. After Truman was born, she thought nothing of leaving him alone, sleeping peacefully in his crib in the Monteleone Hotel, while she went out shopping with friends. But as he grew, so did his demands. He was awake more. He needed more attention. He needed his mother.

Nonetheless, she continued the practice of leaving him, now locking him (sometimes screaming) in a closet so she could go out. In later years he remembered being abandoned there, desperately banging on the door to get out, all the while screaming at the top of his lungs. Lillie Mae also felt trapped and desperate. She wanted a career, a new way of life, and freedom from the responsibility of mothering. By this time there was no marriage, so she separated from Arch and filed for divorce.

When Lillie Mae arrived in Monroeville with Truman for an indefinite stay, she reasoned that Jenny had plenty of room. A parlor, dining room, large kitchen, bathroom, and several bedrooms with double beds in each one served the family well. Each room had a fireplace and high ceilings. But Jenny wasn't interested in having long-term guests. She insisted that Lillie Mae cook and clean to earn her keep. Lillie Mae stayed only a few months, then hocked her diamond rings to Jenny for some money and took off for New York to find a job.

She left Truman behind. Several years later she married Joseph Capote, a wealthy Cuban Catholic whose family wasn't overjoyed at the fact that their son was marrying a divorced country girl with a child. Joe, however, expressed his love by showering Lillie Mae with expensive gifts, taking her on trips abroad, adopting Truman, and sending him to private schools at home and abroad.

When Truman first went to Monroeville in 1928, the yard was walled in by a wooden picket fence. Later Jenny had it torn down to make way for a four-foot-tall fence made of limestone rocks gathered from a nearby creek. The fence, colloquially known as Horse-Bone Rock, was stacked into a form, cemented, then capped with smooth cement. In places the rock sides looked like hunks of animal hip bones poking out.

Inside the house a strange jumble of personalities fused

together as tightly as the fence rocks. It was a family entangled with one another, with members adopting various roles for self-preservation. Like the rock fence she had so painstakingly overseen, Jenny was the bulwark. A spinster, she had earned the respect of male businessmen in the community. But at home, she was Verena, as Truman would later portray her in *The Grass Harp*—"too like a lone man in a house full of women and children, and the only way she could make contact with us was through assertive outbursts: Dolly, get rid of that kitten, you want to aggravate my asthma? Who left the water running in the bathroom? Which of you broke my umbrella? Her ugly moods sifted through the house like a sour yellow mist."

Within Truman's immediate family circle was a first cousin, Jennings Faulk Carter, "Big Boy," whose mother, Mary Ida, was Lillie Mae's sister. Big Boy spent summers and winter weekends at Jenny's house, where he and Truman were inseparable. Their other close playmate was a rough 'n' tough tomboy who lived next door to Jenny's house. She had short, cropped hair, wore coveralls, went barefoot, and could talk mean like a boy. Her name was Nelle Harper Lee, and she was to remain a lifelong friend. A hedge separated the two houses, and Truman, Big Boy, and Nelle slipped through gaps in the hedge to visit back and forth. Mostly it was Nelle at Jenny's house, where they told fantasy tales with Sook (Truman and Jennings Faulk's eccentric cousin), snacked on tea cakes and coffee in the kitchen, and romped and played away precious childhood hours.

Sook was Jenny's eldest sister, a childlike woman who probably suffered from agoraphobia, an abnormal fear of being in public places. She concocted herbal medicine from a secret recipe given to her years earlier by her mother, Samantha. Samantha got the recipe from some Gypsies after she dared enter their camp in the midst of a terrible illness, nursed some of them back to health, and helped bury those who didn't make it. The recipe was the only possession Sook could claim as hers alone.

Sook later became for Truman the pathetic but determined Dolly Talbo, pleading with her equally determined sister, Verena, in *The Grass Harp,* who insists upon having the secret recipe: "You are my own flesh, and I love you tenderly; in my heart I love you. I could prove it now by giving you the only thing that has ever been mine: then you would have it all. Please, Verena," she said, faltering, "let this one thing belong to me."

Although Truman painted an idyllic portrait of Sook in his writings, she was different in real life. In her early years she owned a carriage and occasionally took it out to dig herbs or visit friends. But in the years Truman lived with her, she had become a recluse hiding in the shadows of the long hallway. If a stranger came, she ducked out of sight. She never went outside the confines of the yard. The farthest she would venture was into the chicken yard to gather eggs, and this was but a few steps from the back door. But like the character Dolly Talbo, Sook had endearing qualities: "About all natural things, Dolly was sophisticated; she had the subterranean intelligence of a bee that knows where to find the sweetest flower: she looked around her and felt what she saw."

Some family members say that Sook had a fever in her childhood, which robbed her of her hair and left her rather simpleminded. Pictures of her in later life show her with hair, however, and family members recall that she was rather quick-minded concerning those things she felt strongly about. It very well may have been that she adopted the role of helpless child so that Jenny would take care of her. Sook was somewhat literate. From the time he was very small, Truman made Sook read the funnies to him. When she stumbled over a difficult word, he'd look it up in his pocket dictionary and together they would figure out the meaning.

Sook's relationship with Truman was very special. She was his nurturer and his friend. It was Sook who claimed Truman in her heart. He was her "Buddy" and she was his "Sookie." Oh, the tales they told! The plans they made! They whipped meringue for banana pudding, baked tea cakes, and claimed the kitchen as their special place. And what a kitchen it was! Collin Fenwick in *The Grass Harp* remembered it, too: "If some wizard would like to make me a present, let him give me a bottle filled with the voices of that kitchen, the ha ha ha and fire whispering, a bottle brimming with its buttery sugary bakery smells. . . ."

Then they dusted and cleaned the house, read comic books, worked jigsaw puzzles, and rocked on the back porch. At night, when the sleepy little boy curled beside his Sookie on the double bed, she stroked his blond hair and told him tales until they drifted off to dream.

Caroline Elizabeth (Callie) Faulk also lived in the Faulk household. For several years Callie taught in a one-room country schoolhouse where she was exposed to a variety of children's learning abilities. In times when Jenny's store struggled, Callie was the one who had a steady income. Jenny insisted that Callie give up her job as a schoolteacher and go into the V. H. & C. E. Faulk Millinery and Notions business with her. Jenny's wishes prevailed.

A generous person, Callie would have seen the budding

genius in young Truman. Each day after the noon meal, she practiced her charity by reading to a blind neighbor, Captain Wash Jones. News of the Depression was on the front page, and lively conversations were sparked by current events. Truman curled up on the sofa beside Callie, looking over her shoulder as she read to Captain Wash. A bright child, Truman quickly caught on, learning to read, too. From her school-teaching days, Callie would have known the dangers in this: Children were not supposed to get too far ahead of their peers back then. It made the others look bad. This was extremely frustrating to Truman who, once he started school, found it painful to sit through slow, dreary lessons when he had been reading newspapers since age five.

Nelle Harper Lee, Truman's next-door neighbor and childhood friend, zeroed in on Truman's predicament after she grew up, using it as a basis for one of Scout's dilemmas in *To Kill a Mockingbird:* "If I didn't have to stay [in school] I'd leave. Jem, that damn lady says Atticus's been teaching me to read and for him to stop it. . . . Miss Caroline caught me writing and told me to tell my father to stop teaching me. . . . We don't write in the first grade, we print. You won't learn to write until you're in the third grade."

The only adult male in the Faulk household was Bud, Jenny's brother, who was fifty-nine when Truman came to live there. He is the one who had rescued Truman's grandfather, Arthur, and brought him home to Samantha after Arthur was orphaned. Bud did a little farming but mostly stayed in his room smoking Green Mountain herb for debilitating asthma. Truman liked Bud, a big talker who called him "little Chappie." Bud was very much like Cousin Randolph in *Other Voices, Other Rooms,* although Truman never claimed so. Rather, he attributed the character of Cousin

Randolph to a combination of two men: one, an elderly, asthmatic invalid he met in Mississippi, who smoked medicinal cigarettes, and another man, "obsessed with death, betrayed passions and unfulfilled talent."

Like Cousin Randolph, "Cousin Bud" was somewhat of a loser. His farm was barely successful, and if it had not been for the help of a colored man, John White, there would have been no cotton crop. He refused to ride in an automobile, opting instead to walk to his fields and back every day. He had lost his health. He coughed, choked, and struggled for air in a cold room because he forbade anyone to light a fire in his bedroom, even in the coldest weather. Why he was like this isn't known. The family merely accepted it as "That's the way Bud is."

He lit Green Mountain herb in a saucer and sniffed it for relief from the asthma. He slept in his clothes because if he were to be up in the night walking the halls, he thought it improper not to be dressed, should one of the women get up. Believing his sisters Jenny, Sook, and Callie needed him, he had long ago given up any hope of marriage and children, and stayed at home to be the "man of the house."

*B*ut what else is known about the influences on the young Truman after his mother and father virtually abandoned him? For the first few years he was in Monroeville they rarely saw him. After Truman went north to school, he saw Lillie Mae more often, but never Arch. Not only was he physically separated from his parents, he was also cut off emotionally. It would be years later, after Truman became famous, that Arch would "remember" that Truman was his son. Truman also never liked his stepfather, Joe Capote. Joe spent money lavishly on Truman and tried to get close to him, but a warm relationship never developed.

What did Truman think about during those early years? What was he like? How did he feel? His writings and interviews reflect an eternal quest for his parents' love and acceptance. He became the Joel Knox of *Other Voices, Other Rooms,* "crazy with questions he wanted answered," as he searched for his father. Joel has enormous expectations that the man would be a *real* father, love him, be with him. But the search leads instead to an invalid, a lunatic, who communicates by throwing a ball. In a desperate cry, Joel (Truman) pleads: "God, let me be loved."

Nelle Harper Lee gives us a glimpse of the little boy, Truman, in the character Dill in *To Kill a Mockingbird.* Dill dressed in "blue linen suits that buttoned to his shirt, his hair was snow white and stuck to his head like duck fluff; he was a year my senior but I towered over him. Beautiful things floated around in his dreamy head. He could read two books to my one, but he preferred the magic of his own inventions. He could add and subtract faster than lightning, but he preferred his own twilight world, a world where babies slept, waiting to be gathered like morning lilies."

Several interviews given by Truman Capote himself in magazines and books also provide glimpses of his youth. He claims to have had a difficult childhood. He was aware of Sook's love for him, but except for "cousins and relatives, there was a great absence of love" in his childhood. He swam and fished with his cousins, wrote stories, kept a journal. But he says sadly, "I never felt I belonged anywhere."

The biography by his aunt Marie (Tiny) Rudisill, published a year before his death, was a tremendous disappointment to Truman. He expressed his dismay in *Conversations with Capote,* saying the book is "all a lie. I promise you. It was mostly a complete lie about me. I never had any relationship with this aunt [Tiny] at all. I scarcely even have the vaguest memory of her."

So what is the truth? What kind of childhood did Truman really have there in the scruffy little town of Monroeville? And why was he drawn back there time and time again even after he was jet-setting around the world with the rich and famous? Born to a new destiny, yes, but he was no less a Southern farm boy—the smell of fresh-mown hay and cow manure lured him back, as did fond memories of his youth spent with his family and close cousin, Jennings Faulk Carter, and their mutual friend and neighbor, Nelle Harper Lee. It was, after all, the only family he had.

Jennings Faulk Carter remembers him as "always the leader who dreamed up schemes for us to get into. He set the stage for these little episodes and played them out to the end. But his quick thinking could lead us out of the schemes just as fast. After an adventure, Truman, Nelle, and I would gather back in the chinaberry tree house in Nelle's backyard, or escape to our other hideout underneath Jenny's house. There we'd have our debriefing. He'd say, 'What would have happened if we had done such and such?' Or 'Big Boy, why did you say that? Nelle, why did you do that?' Though we didn't know it at the time, all of this was training leading him to develop as a writer, the same as a dancer develops muscles."

Truman remembered childhood and teenage adventures that later formed the basis of some of his most acclaimed writing. Consider, for example, the tree house. As the place of refuge for the little band of outcasts in *The Grass Harp,* it was "a double-trunked Chinatree, really two trees, but their branches were so embraced that you could step from one into the other; in fact, they were bridged by a tree house."

In later years, during the summer Big Boy worked with his father and two Negro helpers in the fields. Then he spent the weekends in town at Jenny's house. During the week, Nelle and Truman often slipped off and walked down the dirt road to Aunt Mary Ida and Uncle Jennings's farmhouse. Nelle was barefoot. Truman always wore sandals. Once there they coaxed Aunt Mary Ida into frying eggs and bacon and making biscuits, and gave Big Boy an excuse to put away his work plowing or slinging weeds.

It was in the Carter house that Truman saw the only normal family role model of parents and child living together under one roof. Even here, however, it is safe to assume that he saw deprivation inextricably linked with "normal" family life. The Carters lived better than most rural farm families in the South in the 1920s and 1930s. Though not poor, they had no electricity or running water. Their lives were ruled by the sun: up at daylight, to bed at dark. Uncle Jennings had a battery-operated radio, and he occasionally listened to one program at night. Kerosene was expensive, and the Carters used it sparingly. Aunt Mary Ida lit one lamp when absolutely necessary.

An outhouse served as a toilet. When Truman spent the night at Big Boy's house, the boys had to haul in water from the well, heat it on the stove, and pour it into a tub in the middle of the bedroom for their bath. The Carters farmed cotton and corn with two mules and a saddle horse, raised vegetables in their household garden, and had cows and chickens. But money was scarce. These were Depression days, and every penny and nickel counted.

The two black families who lived on the farm occupied

one-room shacks without electricity, running water, or even an outhouse. One of the Negro women, Bama, helped Mary Ida in the kitchen and with her garden. The Negro field hands ate their main meal at noon on a small table in Mary Ida's kitchen. The Carters ate at the big table. This is where Truman entertained them, sometimes during the entire noon meal, with some adventure he'd had at school. "We were spellbound," remembers Jennings Faulk. "We knew it would have to be made-up, but we didn't care. It was all so interesting and he made it sound so real."

It was here out in the country in the little area known as Drewry that Truman got to see the face of real poverty. Sometimes after their meals, there was food left to send to the black women and children who scrounged the woods looking for food to add to their diet of cornbread and milk. A tortoise roasted on the coals, some fish from the creek, or an occasional squirrel flavored the stew pot. Many a night Bama served her family a dish of pepper stew—flour browned in grease, with salt, pepper, and water added.

It was here on the Carter farm that Truman had black friends. Edison McMillan and Charlie McCants were often along when Truman, Big Boy, and their neighbors Buddy Ryland and Dick Carter (no relation) fished, swam, rode mules, told tales, and played boyish pranks. In these later years, Truman and Big Boy realized that their childhood friend Nelle was a female, so she wasn't with them too much during their teenage adventures.

The town of Monroeville was strictly segregated in those days, with the Negroes living in the Clausell quarters. But out in the country, where the Carters lived, most of the Negroes were tenant farmers living on the farm where they worked, and children mixed at work and play.

That Truman lacked a positive male role model, except for his Uncle Jennings, is an understatement. Virtually abandoned by his parents, he saw no marriages at Jenny's house. There were no positive role models in the neighbors, either. On one side of Jenny's house lived Captain and Mrs. Wash Jones. He was a blind ex-military man who daily fought Yankees and demons, and got around as best he could with a cane. She was an invalid in a wheelchair, eternally screeching at her husband for things she needed.

Neighbors on the other side were the Lees, where Nelle was the youngest of three children. Mrs. Lee was considered eccentric, judged by her habit of arising around 2:00 A.M., sitting before the big upright piano, and banging out tunes that in the summer months could be heard all the way to the downtown square.

Truman, however, felt a strong attachment toward Mr. Lee, who tried to spend as much time with his children as possible, but was preoccupied by his work as an attorney, legislator, and editor of the newspaper. Mr. Lee also worked crossword puzzles voraciously. As a child, Truman sat near him, looking over his shoulder, fascinated at the way letters strung together would become words. And Mr. Lee, a man who stressed learning and education, took time with Truman in the evening. They made a game out of finding just the right letters to make words. It was Mr. Lee who gave Truman the cherished little dictionary that Truman religiously carried around in his pants pocket as a youth.

Behind the Lee home was a shack where Anna Stabler lived. She was a mulatto and, reportedly, the illegitimate daughter of a local judge. Without "connections" to the white community, she would have been banished to Clausell. Since she had no teeth, she stuffed cotton in her jaws to help fill out her sagging cheeks. She stayed drunk on bootleg whiskey, twanged her banjo, and sang when she pleased. Truman was as fascinated by her as he was by Sook. Anna was the model for Catherine in *The Grass Harp:* "She lived in the back yard in a tin-roofed silvery little house set among sunflowers and trellises of butterbean vine. She claimed to be an Indian, which made most people wink, for she was dark as the angels of Africa. . . . Most of her teeth were gone; she kept her jaws jacked up with cotton wadding. . . ."

Down the street lived the Boular family. Their son, a recluse, stayed hidden away in the house. Here was a real live "bogeyman" living within hollering distance of Truman's bedroom window. Like Truman, Nelle Lee was fascinated by this character, probably using him as the model for Boo Radley in *To Kill a Mockingbird.*

Such was the hodgepodge of people immediately surrounding the impressionable child. Jenny, Sook, Bud, the Carters, Nelle, and Anna, among others, found themselves in his stories.

Truman claims that he felt lonely and isolated as a child, feelings not uncommon for abandoned, rootless children. But from the time he set foot in Monroeville, he was loved, at least for a few years, until he had played out his role as a dependent, helpless child who needed nurturing and shelter. Sook adored him. Even Jenny cared for him. Although his aunt, Mary Ida, was married, she found some time for him in her home. He had friends and playmates, and enjoyed the role of "idol" to his pals Nelle and Big Boy.

As long as Truman was small, dependent, and helpless, the Faulks would nurture and love him, even if his mother would not. That was their family trait. But the little boy had to grow up and become a man. His writing became the "merciless master." And as he grew into manhood, one by one, almost everyone around him eventually rejected him and his life-style. He tried on many occasions to win back a place for himself within the close family circle, but it seems the harder he tried, the greater the gulf grew between them.

As a consequence, Truman became vindictive at times and found ways to lash back. "His memory was very long," says Jennings Faulk Carter.

The rejection by Sook was perhaps the hardest to take. Poignantly, he tries to recapture their life together in "A Christmas Memory." When she rejects him, he feels it as surely as if he were feeling her death: "I know it. A message saying so merely confirms a piece of news some secret vein had already received, severing from me an irreplaceable part of myself, letting it loose like a kite on a broken string. That is why, walking across a school campus on this particular December morning, I keep searching the sky. As if I expected to see, rather like hearts, a lost pair of kites hurrying toward heaven."

Even if no one but Nelle, Big Boy, Sook, and Callie were aware of it, Truman knew early on that he was different. He thought different. He acted different. The genius was already there, seeking avenues of expression. And even as a very young child he saw those closest to him inventing themselves, adopting roles to play life's game. Sook, Bud, Jenny, Callie, the neighbors, and his mother were playing strange roles. It is no wonder he says, "I invented myself, then a world to fit me."

Early on, Jennings Faulk Carter knew the path Truman was set to travel. Truman began inventing himself in their childhood, and he staged a world to fit himself through their adventures. He knew his goal as a writer and what he had to do to attain it. Jennings Carter recalls, "I remember late one summer, after Truman had returned from Switzerland, he came home to visit Sook and Jenny. I went to see him as soon as I knew he was in town. He was propped up in Sook's big old feather bed. We greeted each other and I sat on the bed and we talked. He was eighteen, just ripe for being drafted. I imagine Lillie Mae and Joe sent him abroad for the summer to get him away, to make sure he wouldn't be drafted.

"I would have joined the army right away, but Jenny talked me out of it. She said, 'Stay and finish high school. The war will last a long time. You'll have plenty of time to fight.'

"At that time I was infuriated with the Japanese and Germans. I said to Truman, 'They're ruining America and will destroy the world!'

"Truman just looked up nonchalantly and said, 'Heroes come and go. Once you're dead, then your world is gone and you'll never experience the things you want to do.'

"By this time I was indignant at Truman for not agreeing with me, so I asked him, 'And what is it that you want to do?'

"He didn't bat an eye when he said, 'Write and read.' "

So it is here in Monroeville that the stage is set. As a collection of childhood adventures, the stories fill an enormous gap in what is known at present about Truman Capote. These adventures, as remembered by Jennings Faulk Carter, not only delight and entertain, but also provide a serious insight into the workings of the mind of one of America's great writers.

The stories begin three years after Lillie Mae deposited Truman at Jenny's house. It is the summer of 1931, a typical day. Sook brought the milk in early, before the sun got too hot. Little moist circles remain on the cement steps where the milk bottles stood an hour ago. Mr. Ralls's new calf, the one he bought to fatten up by winter, is bellowing at the top of its lungs. Mr. Ralls has thrown a tub full of dry corn over the fence, but the calf hasn't found it yet. Some blue jays are squawking in the top of Nelle's tree house. Captain and Mrs. Jones have had their first spat of the day; now she has rolled her wheelchair out on the front porch to pout.

Jenny and Callie have walked downtown to their mercantile store. They took a parasol today to shade their white faces from the hot, bright June sun. Bud has left early for his fields, walking as always. The cook is outside washing turnip greens to prepare for dinner.

A shirtless, barefooted Big Boy is visiting Truman at Jenny's house. He's wearing the dark brown shorts he slept in last night. Truman has on pressed shorts and shirt, socks and sandals. Nelle, in cut-off coveralls and no shirt on her tanned back, pushes aside a limb of green hedge and joins Truman and Big Boy on the front porch steps. The children sniff tea cakes cooking on the wood stove. Their eyes brighten when they think of Sook dipping fresh cookies in hot coffee, and they scamper into the kitchen to look for her.

# Sook's Secret

*A woman with shorn white hair is standing at the kitchen window. She is wearing tennis shoes and a shapeless gray sweater over a summery calico dress. She is small and sprightly, like a bantam hen; but, due to a long youthful illness, her shoulders are pitifully hunched. Her face is remarkable—not unlike Lincoln's, craggy like that, and tinted by sun and wind; but it is delicate, too, finely boned, and her eyes are sherry-colored and timid. . . .*

*She is sixty-something. We are cousins, very distant ones, and we have lived together—well, as long as I can remember. Other people inhabit the house, relatives; and though they have power over us and frequently make us cry, we are not, on the whole, too much aware of them. We are each other's best friend.*

TRUMAN CAPOTE, "A Christmas Memory"

*W*hen Truman Capote and I were children [recalls Jennings Faulk Carter], we always thought of Sook as our friend. Unlike the other adults who scolded, ruled, and otherwise tried to mold us into something *they* thought we should be, Sook was different. She let us be children, because in her own way she was as much a child as we were.

Born Nanny Rumbley Faulk in 1871 she was, as Truman wrote, sixty-something when we were children spending time with her in the 1930s and 1940s. I spent almost as much time with Sook and Truman at Jenny's house as I did at my parents' farm about two miles down Drewry Road. Being with Sook meant fun and games, and I could hardly wait to get there.

Sook was not only our friend but the nearest thing we had to a grandmother. She was kind, loving, and giving. Jenny and Callie liked telling Truman and me stories about Sook in her younger years when she'd hitch up old Sam, the horse, and go for buggy rides over dirt roads to visit her country friends. Even winter weather wouldn't stop her. She'd bundle up and wrap wool scarves around her hands to keep them warm.

But by the time Truman and I were born in the mid-1920s, Sook had become a recluse. I never knew her to leave the yard even to go to church on Sunday. No, on Sunday she read her Bible, folded her hands for a prayer, and then looked up with a radiance that let us know she'd been somewhere special.

She was content to stay at the house, which was practically walled in by this big limestone-rock fence. She picked peas and beans in the backyard garden or went to the wash house where the colored woman washed the clothes every week. One of Sook's daily chores was gathering eggs from the henhouse. Always at her side was her little pet terrier, Queenie. In spite of her sisters' disdain over the matter of chewing tobacco, Sook chewed discreetly, even carrying around a little handkerchief to wipe her mouth.

A barber came over to the house once a month to cut Sook's sparse, white hair to below her ears. A high fever when she was a child had left her almost bald, with an enlarged heart and suffering from rheumatism. The fever may have accounted for her shy personality as well, for she had a shyness that was almost painful, except with children.

Her sisters showed her little respect, treating her more

like their servant than a sister. She did the ironing and cleaned the house, and if anyone in the family was sick, she nursed them back to health. I've seen her tear dirty sick linens off the bed and boil them with the sick clothes in a black wash-pot over an open fire in the backyard, then string them on the line to dry in the sun. When Callie and Jenny came in tired and irritable from working all day in their store, Sook was supposed to be pleasant to them and never argue back, even when they grumbled to her. Another of her duties was telling the cook what to do, as well as doing a lot of the baking. She made light, lemony, tea-cake cookies. Truman, Nelle, and I loved to sit in the kitchen with Sook after she made a fresh pot of coffee and a batch of cookies. She dipped the cookies in the hot coffee to soften them to make it easier for her to chew with her dentures. She did the same for us, feeding us one at a time.

We'd laugh and talk about things that were important to us, like the way old Miz Katz fattened her Christmas goose by holding it down and stuffing corn in its mouth until its long neck couldn't hold another kernel.

Sometimes Jenny would burst in on the scene and start yelling, "Don't give those children coffee! Don't you know it's bad for them? Silly old woman!" Then Sook's eyes would fill with tears, and she'd shrug her shoulders, purse her lips, and lead us quickly outside—anything to avoid a row with Jenny.

Her only reward was being able to play with her young friends, Truman, Nelle, and me. Sometimes she called Truman Buddy; they called me Big Boy. Truman was Sook's dearest, and Nelle and I knew it, but that was all right because she had enough love to go around. We especially liked Sunday afternoons after the grown-ups had finished reading the newspaper, the *Mobile Register*. We'd take the comics and crawl up on Sook in her rocking chair on the back porch and read for hours. "Hambone" was one of our favorites. Helped along by Sook and Callie, Truman could read even before he started to school. He'd read "Hambone" in a deep voice, sounding for all the world like John White, the colored man who worked for Sook's brother, Bud, in the fields. Truman also had a high, squeaky voice, and when he mocked the characters we'd laugh until our sides ached. Then Sook would wrap her wiry arms around us and squeeze us with all her might, especially Truman.

Truman needed extra love and affection in those days. After his mother, Lillie Mae, moved to New York and left Truman behind, she made no secret of her feelings. She wrote letters and cried over the telephone to Truman about how she had no money and no husband. Truman would cry to Sook, and then Sook would cry and say, "Oh, Buddy, I don't know what we can do to help our Lillie Mae get some money and be happy."

Sook loved Lillie Mae, too, for she had helped raise Lillie Mae, my mother, Mary Ida, and their sister, Marie, when their parents died. Now she was raising Lillie Mae's little son. So to ease Truman's woes about his mother leaving him and then telling him how miserable she was, Sook dedicated herself to trying to make him happy. She was the center of his world. Mine, too, especially when we played pretend games. That's when Truman would sit on Sook's lap, and Nelle and I'd climb on each arm of the rocking chair. Sook would wrap her arms around us cocoonlike. We'd talk for hours, making up all kinds of stories. Truman could outdo Sook in the stories, even when he was six or seven years old. We'd lose ourselves in an adventure of killing a giant lizard, thus saving this beautiful, dark-haired young girl who, for some reason, always looked just like Lillie Mae. And we'd kill the lizard carefully, never cutting off his tail lest another one would grow in its place.

Or maybe we just escaped some horrid Indian massacre like the one fought years ago at nearby Burnt Corn, Alabama, when Sook would suddenly shriek and say, "Oh! Oh! Callie and Jenny'll be here any minute. Dear Lord in heaven, is the commode flushed? The stove top clean? Dinner on the table?" She'd pop up and rush around tidying up before the stern-faced sisters arrived, or else face a tongue-lashing for sure.

Each evening Jenny brought the money sack home from the store. She plopped the drawstring sack filled with loose change and bills on the desk in her room or hung it on the bedpost. When Jenny and Callie were in the living room listening to a radio program after supper, and Sook thought no eyes were watching, she would reach into the sack, slip out a handful of change, and drop it into her apron pocket. She never bothered the bills. Then when Truman, Nelle, and I were there playing games, she'd stick her hand down into her apron pocket, pull up three nickels, and say, "My, oh my. Look what I found here. Why Buddy, here's one for you. And one for Big Boy and Nelle, too."

She always saved back enough change for her special treat, Brown Mule Chewing Tobacco. She'd get us to go to town and buy it for her. We loved doing this because we felt all grown up when we went shopping for Sook, handing the money to the clerk and saying, "One plug of Brown Mule, please." Then we'd take our nickels to the drugstore and splurge on candy or a soda. Sometimes we'd charge our sodas to Jenny's account; she never complained.

Sook was never paid for any of her work around the house. Nor did she reap any monetary benefit from the land her father had left her. Her brother, Bud, took over her land and made it part of his cotton farm. Her clothes came from the racks in Jenny and Callie's store or secondhand from her sisters. She had no assets of her own. But she did have one thing that was hers and hers alone—a secret recipe for rheumatism medicine. Sook's mother, Samantha Rumbley, got the recipe from a band of Gypsies who came to town horse-trading before the Civil War. They camped out at the old horse-racing track near Monroeville. While they had their tent and wagon camping ground set up, they came down with a fever that nearly wiped them out. Although many of the people in Monroeville were reluctant to enter the camp for fear of the fever and fear of the Gypsies themselves, Samantha, who lived nearby, heard their moans and wails. She went into the camp and nursed the Gypsies. She helped them bury their dead in Emmons New Ground Cemetery.

To show her appreciation, an old Gypsy woman gave the medicine recipe to Samantha. It was a concoction of natural ingredients, which supposedly eased the pain of rheumatism and gout. Samantha made the medicine by boiling the roots of the sourwood tree, mixing this with iron filings, and adding two secret ingredients. She strained the syrup through fine muslin, then bottled and aged it. There was a ritual for taking the medicine. Patients had to take a certain amount per day and had to adhere to a strict dietary regimen: no salt, fatty foods, or foods cooked in grease for as long as they took the medicine. Now all this was easier said than done, for most of the foods eaten by country folks back then were full of salt and fat. Meat, especially pork, was cured in salt as a preservative to make salt pork, a flavoring for turnips, collards, peas, and squash. And hog lard was the staple fat in everything else, from corn bread and biscuits to fried chicken.

Before Samantha died she gave Sook, and only Sook, the secret recipe. I don't know why she told only Sook, or why it was such a secret. Perhaps she thought Sook needed something that was hers alone to bring her some income. After all, Callie and Jenny had the store, and Bud had the farm.

Sook's fame spread as the one with a cure for rheumatism, and people came from all over Alabama to buy the dark, sticky liquid. Her business thrived so much that the doctors and druggists sicced the sheriff on her to shut down the operation. But nothing stopped Sook.

As Sook got up in age, Jenny and Callie hired colored men to go into the woods to gather sourwood roots and bring in the iron filings. From there she could manage. She cooked her concoction in a large black pot in the backyard, stirring and sniffing all day. Then she'd strain it and pour it in medicine bottles obtained from the drugstore. Sook booked appointments for her patients with Jenny or Callie. Sook had a large clientele of coloreds, but not exclusively.

When her patients arrived, they went to the back door because coloreds just didn't go to the front door in those days. They stood close to the back steps in the sunlight and called, "Miss Nanny, are you in there?" From the shadows at the center of the house, Sook answered, "I'm here," then proceeded to ask questions: "Where's the swelling? Do you have any sores? How long have you had them? Do they hurt?"

The patients rolled up a pants leg and showed swollen joints, or pulled back a sweater to show a sore on an arm. Sook looked critically, rubbed her chin, thought about it, but never touched anyone. Once she was satisfied, she emerged from the shadows, handed over the medicine, and took the dollar. "Now swear you won't eat any salt or fatty food, and that you'll take the medicine every day," she said.

"Yessum, Miss Nanny, jest like you say," was the reply.

One day Sook, Truman, Nelle, and I were sitting on the back porch killing off giant lizards in a pretend game. Sook went inside to her bedroom to take a spoonful of rheumatism medicine and when she came back outside, her face was flushed with excitement. "Oh, Buddy! I have it! I know how Lillie Mae can get rich. Then she won't be so worried about finding a new husband. Come quick!" She grabbed Truman by the hand and told Nelle and me to wait there. Then the two hurried down the steps to the shade of the pecan tree. They put their heads together. Nelle and I strained our eyes and ears trying to see and hear what they were saying. But we couldn't make out a word. It sure looked serious, though. Sook took a stick in her hand and drew something in the dirt. She'd talk, then Truman would talk. Then she'd talk more, and Truman would answer. They seemed to stay out there forever. Finally, Sook, all smiles, kissed Truman's cheek and seemed to walk on air as she went around toward the front of the house out of our sight.

Nelle and I descended on Truman, our bare feet hardly touching the smooth wooden steps. "Tell us what Sook said! Tell us the secret!" But for the first time in his life, Truman was reluctant to talk. He grinned sheepishly.

There's no pretending that Nelle and I didn't feel hurt and left out, because we did. "Sook gave you the secret formula, didn't she? *Didn't she?*" we insisted.

Truman looked at us as though he wanted to say something but was carefully choosing his words. His bright eyes darted first to me, then to Nelle, then to the room where he knew his beloved Sook was stretched out on her bed taking an afternoon nap. He dropped his head and thought a moment before he spoke. "Big Boy and Nelle, you know you're my best friends in all the world—next to Sook," he began. "Sook knew something that only she knew, and now I know it, too. But I can never, never tell."

And I doubt he ever did.

# 2
# Miss Jenny's Halloween Party

*It was a memory, a childish memory of terrors that once, long ago, had hovered above like haunted limbs on a tree of night. Aunts, cooks, strangers—each eager to spin a tale or teach a rhyme of spooks and death, omens, spirits, demons. And always there had been the unfailing threat of the wizard man: stay close to the house, child, else a wizard man will snatch you and eat you alive! He lived everywhere, the wizard man, and everywhere there was danger. At night, in bed, hear him tapping at the window? Listen!*

TRUMAN CAPOTE, "A Tree of Night"

$S$hortly after Truman began the second grade, he received a letter from his mother saying she was going to marry Joe Capote [a wealthy Cuban living in New York]. Lillie Mae said for him not to plan on finishing the year in Monroeville, because she and Joe wanted to enroll him in a boarding school up North. This was not at all pleasing to Truman, who cried and didn't want to go. Eventually reconciled to the fact that he would be leaving, he decided to celebrate by giving a party. "One that will be so much fun and so exciting that people in Monroeville will remember me and the party forever," he said to Nelle and me.

Truman's first step was convincing Jenny to let him have the party on a Friday night, which was unheard of because no child in Monroeville ever had a party at night. Children had parties during the daylight hours. Some of the children lived several miles from town, and a nighttime party meant that their parents would have to drive to town over unlit dirt roads, then find something to do to amuse themselves until the party was over. Afterward, they had to drive back over the same dangerous route.

But Truman pleaded with Jenny to include the adults so he could be sure of a large gathering of children. "The adults can have refreshments and listen to the new Victrola in the living room while we children have our party in the back-yard," Truman said convincingly. In all her sixty years, Jenny had never had a party, although she was a frequent guest at many an afternoon tea in Monroeville. She had been so busy trying to make a living at the mercantile store, her only planned entertaining was on Sundays at noon, when the preacher or some other special guests came to eat Sook's famous deep-dish chicken pie.

Jenny thought the party was a grand idea, and she helped Truman plan a guest list to include some of her "better" customers, along with important townspeople like the mayor and his wife and the probate judge. For once in their lives, Truman and Jenny were on the same brain wave. Though Jenny and Truman's relationship was one of toleration bro-ken by occasional bouts of quarreling over such "memory lapses" as Truman's forgetting to water the flowers, *this* time they were seeing things eye to eye. "Everyone must come in costume, and Jenny and I will judge who has the best costume. There will be a prize for the winner," Truman said. Jenny even liked that idea. She already had the prizes— some rancid chocolate bars left over at the store from last Christmas.

Since nothing much went on in the little country town, word quickly spread around the school and throughout the community about the wonderful Halloween party planned at Jenny's house. Everybody wanted to be included. Parents who hadn't been in Jenny's store in months came to see Miss Jenny (as they respectfully called her) to hint for an invitation to the party. The list grew long.

Truman had one person he especially wanted to invite— a black man named John White. John often helped Truman's cousin, Bud Faulk, with his farm chores, and when Truman approached him about helping at the party, John was thrilled to be included. So thrilled, in fact, that he told everybody, "*I'm* gonna be at Miss Jenny's party."

It's just this kind of remark, even made in innocence, that spreads like boot blacking on a clean white floor in little towns like Monroeville. John didn't know he was doing anything wrong by mentioning his special status. The same cannot be said for Truman. It was Truman who thought about soot-black John the day he went into Jenny's store and saw a man's white suit hanging on the racks. Truman planned to dress John in the suit and a white hat. "He'll look just like a ghost," Truman said. "He'll stand by the storage shed behind the wash tubs filled with apples for bobbing."

Now these weren't just ordinary, home-grown apples. These were Sook's special, giant, Red Delicious apples shipped in from Washington State. Jenny ordered them through a wholesale house. Every autumn a wooden crate arrived filled with the big red apples wrapped in tissue. Sook had false teeth, so she didn't dare try to chomp down on an apple. Instead, she cut the apple, scraped the soft, white meat with a blunt knife, and ate the pulp. A favorite pastime for Truman, Nelle, and me was perching like hungry baby birds on Sook's rocking chair on the back porch and eating scraped apple from her fingers.

Truman knew he had to have some of those apples, but to get them, he'd have to do some strong persuading. "They're so big that even if somebody gets one pressed against the side of the tub, they can't bite it."

Sook laughed. "Oh, Buddy!" she exclaimed. "You've thought of everything."

While we talked with Sook about the guest list for the party, Nelle remembered that we had forgotten to invite Sally Boular and her brother, Sonny. The Boular house sat on the corner next to the school yard, about half a block from the Lee and Faulk houses. A fence of fruit trees, a scuppernong arbor, and wire surrounded the house. The Boulars didn't seem to want anybody in—or out. Sally Boular was a friendly, bright young woman who clerked in one of the stores downtown. She walked by the Faulk and Lee houses each day, waved, and talked to Nelle, Truman, and me. But Sonny was something else entirely. He was a tall, thin young man with a face so pale he looked almost ghostly, leading some of our friends to develop a legend about him: Sonny's dangerous and if he ever gets out of his yard, he'll kill you with a butcher knife.

There was nothing too wrong with Sonny except that he was kept at home and was enormously shy. No one had ever seen him leave his yard. Nelle, who wasn't afraid of anything, had dared to be friendly with Sonny. Once she and I stood at the edge of his yard and she talked to him while he sat on the front porch. Nothing bad happened. Sonny didn't have a murderous look in his eye, and he didn't try to attack anybody.

When Nelle brought up the subject of inviting Sonny and Sally to the party, everyone agreed it was a good idea. "After all, they are neighbors," Jenny said.

Another of Jenny's neighbors was the feared and respected Sheriff Farrish, a huge man who wore a khaki uniform, tall boots, and a shining badge over his heart. He kept a long revolver thrust into a heavy black holster around his waist. Anybody who saw him knew he meant business, and he did. Supposedly, he had killed several people—Indians, whites, and black men—although nobody knew exactly how many.

A few days before the party, the sheriff drove up in front of Jenny's house in an old patrol car, the kind with a windshield that rolled out. The car had a siren mounted on the window post, and the sheriff had to reach outside with his left arm to crank it. He wired the siren handle down, and with good reason. He learned the hard way that the handle was the first thing kids ran for when they saw the car parked downtown. Many a shopper walking along with packages dropped them in mortal fright when a child grabbed the siren handle and let out a blast loud enough to wake the dead.

On this warm autumn day, Jenny came out the front gate to see what the sheriff wanted. She wore a pink cotton dress, white shoes that laced, and her gray hair twirled around in a bun on top of her head. Once considered the town beauty, she still had an elegant carriage about her that commanded respect. The sheriff stood by his car, almost at attention, as though he dreaded saying what he had to say, particularly to her. Nelle, Truman, and I slipped around the fence, ran up beside the car, and crouched on the dusty black running board to hear the sheriff's words.

"Morning, Miss Jenny," he said, tipping his hat, then putting it back on his head to make sure everything was all official.

"What brings you out to see me?" Jenny asked.

The sheriff cleared his throat, looked down, and started talking. He told her the talk around town was that Master Truman invited some Negroes to his party. "Now I don't believe it's true, but a lot of people do. The talk is that he plans to *show* the people in Monroeville a thing or two before he goes up North."

By this time, Jenny had her arms on her hips and her jaws clenched. "Mmmm," she said, nodding curtly. "Go on."

"Well, ma'am, as I understand the talk, Master Truman's plan is that the coloreds will come dressed in costumes that nobody can identify. Nobody will know they're coloreds until after the party is over, and the damage will have been done. Now Miss Jenny, this talk has got the Klan all riled up. They're even planning a meeting in the school yard the night of the party. I have already stopped by Anna Stabler's house and told her to spend the night with some of her kin in Clausell that night."

Anna was the colored woman who lived in a shack near the school. I couldn't imagine what all this had to do with Anna, but I did know that any mention of the Klan meant trouble.

The sheriff went on to explain that the Klan hadn't had any excitement in a long time and the Klansmen were beginning to lose interest in being in the organization. "They won't attend meetings and pay dues if nothing is going on, and this gets the chief Dragon upset. So he's planned a show of strength. After their meeting in the school yard, they plan to march down Alabama Avenue in front of your house. Now I've told them not to say or throw anything, but to be quiet and not interrupt your party."

Jenny was furious. She pointed a finger in the sheriff's

face as she spewed out her words. "Some Grand Dragon! The gall of him! I'll snatch him bald. You can go tell him to send his old biddie of a wife to pay her store bill. I've been carrying her on my books for years now, and *this* is how he repays me? By criticizing my family? Threatening me? And as for you, sheriff, the last time that worthless bunch of no-'count Klansmen raised cain in Monroeville, it was all over nothing. And you know it was. They had all that trouble with the colored boy and were threatening to hang him. Why all they had to do was ask that little white hussy he was accused of molesting . . ."

Realizing she was saying too much to be ladylike, she stopped. Then she remembered something else. "I'll say this much," she continued. "You know how loose that girl is. The colored boy should have known better. All he did was talk to her. Just talk. The Klan got all excited and wanted to hang him. You should have stepped in and stopped the thing right then and there."

"Now Miss Jenny, I would have tried to stop it if I had felt that the boy was worth saving. You know what a trial and tribulation he was. He wouldn't work for anybody. He was impudent as he could be. The Klan did some good with him. They put the fear of the Lord in him and he went up to Detroit where he belongs. As for that hussy, if she keeps being so brazen, I'll have to see that she moves her business to Mobile."

Jenny Faulk had one last word on the matter. "There won't be any funny business under my roof, not under the Faulk roof. Do you understand me? I don't need to remind you of your duties, now do I? Or of the fact that I contributed heavily to your campaign? Good day, sheriff."

With that, she tramped back into the house, the red-faced

sheriff drove off in a cloud of dust, and we scampered into Nelle's tree house.

I had one question burning on my brain. "What's a hussy?"

Truman took out his little pocket dictionary and thumbed through it. "It's not in here," he said. "Besides, you know what a hussy is, Big Boy."

I said I didn't know.

"Well," Truman said, "a hussy's a hussy."

With that question settled, we planned the games and guests, food and fun we would have at the party. We wondered if the Klan would spoil the party, but decided that Jenny had taken care of that.

The day of the party finally arrived. Truman talked Bud and his uncle Frank into building a track from the back-porch stoop down to the ground beneath the pecan tree. The men agreed to build a rail that the wheels of Truman's tricycle airplane would fit in so the plane would scoot down the steps and roll onto the ground. Truman said that if only the plane would go faster, it would fly, and we believed him.

Nelle and I knew if we could help Truman think of enough games for the other children to play, then we would have more times to ride the airplane down the track. Nelle convinced her brother, Ed, to loan his air rifle for the balloon shoot. Bud built a wooden spinning-arm attached to a backboard. He blew up red and yellow balloons with pennies and nickels in each one, then tied them to the rotating arm. As he turned the arm, the boys and girls aimed at the spinning balloons from a distance of about ten feet back. *Pop!* And a penny or nickel rolled to the floor, a true prize in Depression days.

There were other games, where the fearless ones put their

hands inside a hole cut in a cardboard box and tried to guess what was inside. One box held a squirming, inverted green tortoise stuck into a form that kept it from turning upright. As it struggled, scratching in the leaves and sticks, the children stuck their hands inside the box and felt the cool, hard, clawing, live monster. No one guessed it was only a tortoise. In another box Truman had placed a bowl of bananas and oranges mashed together in a glob. Most people felt the gooey substance and said "chitlins." [Chitterlings is a dish of cooked pig intestines.] The third box held a turkey-wing duster. Most people knew this right away because they had feather dusters at home.

Some of the grown-ups entered into the fun, too. Callie planned to come dressed as a bride. "When Jenny and I judge the costume contest, we'll judge the very best devil and you can marry the devil," Truman said to his attractive older cousin, who had never wed.

Knowing that at least a hundred people would show up for the party, Jenny planned accordingly for refreshments. The adults would be inside the house with punch in pretty glass cups and molasses cookies served on the mahogany sideboard. The children would have divinity candy, pulled molasses candy, little cakes, and punch served in "newfangled paper cups" outside beneath the pecan trees. Jenny bought outdoor lights and had them installed so the entire yard would be flooded in light from front to back.

When the night of the party arrived, Nelle and I painted our faces with red lipstick and chimney soot and pulled on some men's shirts to hide our cut-off shorts. Truman had gone all out, painting his face yellow, then adding a brown mustache like Fu Manchu. Truman avidly read the newspapers every day, and probably was influenced by reports of

Chinese Tong wars in California that were going on at the time. Sook had made his outfit, a buttoned-up coat with a straight collar, and a shirt hanging over loose trousers. He pinned a skullcap to his blond hair. He talked John White into clipping enough hair from a neighbor's mule tail to plait a pigtail, which he pinned inside his cap to hang down his back.

As the guests arrived, Truman and Jenny greeted them at the door, and Truman wrote in his notebook a number according to the merit of each costume. There were devils, ghosts, dragons, witches, and Callie the bride. The adults played Chinese checkers, drank punch, and listened to records on Jenny's phonograph. It played only one record at a time and had to be rewound after each song, but it was an amazing piece of entertainment that few people in Monroeville had ever seen or heard.

The children lined up to shoot at the balloons with Ed's air rifle. Another group bobbed for apples or stuck their hands inside the boxes and tried to guess the mystery ingredients. Since so many of the children were anxious to play those games, they ignored the tricycle airplane. With two strong men to haul the little plane up the steps after each flight down, Nelle and I flew to our heart's content, which was something we never would have been able to do otherwise. On other days, Truman was notoriously selfish with his toy plane.

By this time, most of the guests had peeked under masks and knew who everybody else was. Everyone was there except Sally and Sonny, who weren't missed in the midst of all the laughter, balloon-popping, and music floating through the warm October night. Even Jenny entered into the laughter and talking, never mentioning the sheriff's visit or giving any more thought to his words. And with all their attention on the party, the adults had failed to notice what was happening down the street in the school yard. One by one, cars pulled up; a white-robed figure would get out and pull a hood over his head that hid all but his eyes. The men spoke softly, lit their torches, and started up the street, walking slowly toward Jenny's house.

The party was in full swing when Sally Boular, dressed in a fluffy princess costume, burst into the house, shrieking, "Help! Please help! The Klan's got Sonny over at Mr. Lee's house! They're gonna hang him!"

She screamed her words as she described what happened. "We got on our costumes and walked as far as the Lees' when the Klan saw us. They yelled, 'There's one of them now!' and started running after us. We got scared and started running. Sonny tripped and fell in Mr. Lee's yard. He couldn't get up. They grabbed him and said they're gonna hang him! Come quick!"

Someone yelled, "Call the sheriff!"

While the adults crowded to the door in a hubbub of activity, Truman, Nelle, and I darted out the back door, down the steps, across the yard, and through the hedge. We reached Nelle's front porch before any of the adults managed to get there. All except Mr. Lee, who had heard the commotion and was standing outside in his undershirt and blue pants. He waded into the middle of the sheet-covered Klansmen, who had gathered in the middle of the road holding their torches high.

The Klansmen didn't offer any resistance to Mr. Lee, a big, strong man who had the respect of everybody in town. He was a member of the state legislature, editor of the *Monroe Journal,* and an upstanding citizen. No one wanted to be the one to cross him. When Mr. Lee got to the center of the activity, he came face-to-face with a Klansman wearing a hood with green fringe. This was the Grand Dragon.

In the center of the group was a series of silver-painted cardboard boxes that had been wired to make a square head, body, arms, and legs. Round eye-holes were cut in the front of the box on the head. The strange figure could barely walk with all the boxes wired to him, and he couldn't get his arms up to pull the box from his head. As Mr. Lee moved close to him, the voice inside the box whimpered and cried out. Mr. Lee grabbed one of the box arms and pulled the man through the crowd of people back up to his porch. With only the light from the Klansman's torch to see by, Mr. Lee proceeded to unwrap the tape that held the box over the head. When he finally removed the box, there was Sonny, white as a sheet, with tears streaming down his face. He tried to cling to Mr. Lee, but the boxes kept him back. "I wasn't going to hurt anybody," he said. "I was coming to the party as a robot, that's all."

Mr. Lee turned to address the crowd of Klansmen. "See what your foolishness has done? You've scared this boy half to death because you wanted to believe something that wasn't true. You ought to be ashamed of yourselves."

Standing behind Mr. Lee was a solid line of the most influential people in Monroeville—the probate judge, county commissioners, the sawmill owner, the bank president, and several big landowners. In short, the power who ran the county gathered there in one final affront to the Klan, who one by one silently ground their torches into the dirt and faded into the blackened night.

Nobody but the family and Nelle went back to Jenny's house. "Where was the sheriff when we needed him?" Jenny asked. We learned later that the sheriff and his deputy had been called out of town. While we discussed the excitement and danger, Truman was getting it all in perspective. Then his comments and questions bubbled out: "Did you see the look on Sonny's face when he was crying? Did you see that he'd shaved? He had a stubble of beard. And how about Mr. Lee? Did you notice after he spoke there was no shouting, no more talk? Did you see the look on the people's faces?" He paused, then said thoughtfully, "The power of the Klan is gone. Nobody has to be afraid of them anymore."

The night was as Truman had predicted: one that people would remember.

AUTHOR'S NOTE:

This Halloween party had special significance for Nelle Harper Lee. Although it would be several decades before she began writing *To Kill a Mockingbird,* the sights, sounds, smells, tension, and drama of that evening made their lasting imprint on her mind, for the climactic scenes in *Mockingbird* occurred at a school yard and on the road home from a Halloween party.

The sympathetic character Boo Radley, a recluse hiding in the shadows, likely was based on Sonny Boular. And the struggle of Scout Finch in a bulky costume constructed of chicken wire and brown cloth that made it nearly impossible for her to see or walk was probably grounded in poor Sonny Boular's trouble that night with his robot costume.

Then there was the conversation about the Klan, the black man, and the hussy—actual events that occurred in Monroeville. The angry lynch mob on Nelle's darkened front porch could have been the lynch mob after poor Tom Robinson, the Negro man unjustly accused in her novel.

The close relationship she enjoyed with her pals Big Boy and Truman was reflected in conversations in *To Kill a Mockingbird* with Scout's brother, Jem, and their friend Dill, the prissy little boy who came to visit next door.

Most of all, when Nelle remembered the bravery and determination of a father so strong that it broke the back of the Klan in Monroeville that night, she created the unforgettable character of Atticus Finch, a lone man crying out for justice.

And to think it all began at Miss Jenny's Halloween party.

# 3
# Orange Beach

*Writing was always an obsession with me, quite simply something I had to do, and I don't understand exactly why this should have been true. It was as if I were an oyster and somebody forced a grain of sand into my shell—a grain of sand that I didn't know was there and didn't particularly welcome. Then a pearl started forming around the grain and it irritated me, made my angry, tortured me sometimes. But the oyster can't help becoming obsessed with the pearl.*

"An Interview with Truman Capote"
*McCall's,* November 1967

$A$long the Gulf Coast of Alabama, Orange Beach was a favorite vacation spot for the Faulk, Capote, and Carter families. When we were kids growing up in the early 1930s, our folks would load up the car with food, linens, and towels. We'd leave early in the morning for the four-hour drive across rough roads until we reached the beach, where we rented a cabin overnight.

There wasn't any air-conditioning in those days. Gulf breezes blew in during the day, and at night we slept under a light blanket. There was something therapeutic about being at the Gulf, away from our regular farm routine. Daddy and Mother were struggling to make it through the Depression, and even Jenny Faulk's mercantile store saw some hard times.

Joe and Lillie Mae would send Truman down to Jenny's house as soon as his school was over for the summer. Later they would drive down from New York in Joe's big black touring car with a steamer trunk strapped on the back. We looked forward to their visit, because this signaled a time of partying and family reunion. Although these were Prohibition times, Joe and Lillie Mae always brought plenty of liquor with them. The Capotes made no secret of their drinking when they came to Jenny's house, even though Sheriff Farrish lived across the street two doors down. He knew they all drank—even Jenny.

Lillie Mae seemed to have everything going for her in those days. She and Joe were very comfortable on Joe's money and private investments, and she had acquired some, if not all, of the social status she thought she should have. Lillie Mae was a beautiful woman with lily-white skin, dark hair, and a figure that put Venus to shame. She probably would have done very well as an actress, because around the family she staged and acted out miniature scenes in order to display herself. For her centerpiece she used some action such as a dinner party, or an object she had bought for the house. Then she'd get so caught up in acting out her part that you felt yourself swept up in it, too. Truman modeled his behavior on hers, right down to the letter. He staged little scenes just like his mother. It was amusing to watch the two of them trying to upstage each other.

On this trip Joe, Truman, and Lillie Mae (Joe called her Nina, which means "little girl"), Mother and Daddy, Jenny Faulk, Nelle, and I crawled into Joe's big car about daybreak on Saturday and headed for Orange Beach. We stopped at a little seafood restaurant somewhere near the coast and ate fresh raw oysters that were shucked as fast as we could get them down. We laughed, thinking we might find a pearl and sell it for lots of money.

It was about noon when we arrived at the cabin, unloaded

our food and clothes, then dressed for an afternoon of fun on the beach. All of us liked the water, but none of us could swim as well as Truman. He'd been swimming since he was barely toddling, mostly in the pool at the Monteleone Hotel in New Orleans, where he lived until he was three.

Back then most country people didn't have special beach clothes or equipment. Jenny waded in a lightweight dress. Mother had a one-piece suit consisting of a short skirt over short pants, with a plain top that didn't dare expose any bosom. The males had cut-off pants, except for Joe and Truman, who wore bright red-and-blue swimming trunks and long-sleeved white beach coats. Nelle had little cut-off coveralls, and at this stage in our childhood, she didn't wear a top. We had tattered quilts to spread on the sand.

Lillie Mae chose a beach umbrella and portable bar to set her scene, along with a knock-your-eyes-out bathing suit. It was yellow, tight-fitting, with elastic in the legs. The top was low and held up her generous bosom with little straps that crossed in back.

When she bent over to tie Truman's beach coat, it was hard to keep your eyes off her ample cleavage. "Isn't Truman adorable in his little swimsuit?" Lillie Mae said, directing her comments to Jenny. "Yes" was all Jenny had to say.

Even at age eight, Truman recognized that his mother's scanty top was going to cause trouble for somebody. He stared at her bosom, then said, "I like your swimsuit, Mother."

Nelle and I didn't care that Truman had new red-and-blue trunks with a drawstring at the waist, and neatly hemmed pants legs. I was happy enough that Jenny had given me a new sand pail painted with flying sea gulls, and a matching spade for digging.

"Is everybody ready to go?" Lillie Mae asked, draping a

yellow-and-blue beach towel over her shoulders. She put on dark glasses and a sun hat with a bright yellow band.

Jenny squashed one of Sook's straw garden hats on her gray hair, looked disapprovingly at Lillie Mae, and said, "Do ya think you're going to a fashion show? That suit is rather *revealing*, Lillie Mae."

"Yes, and isn't it grand? I bought it in New York. Joe was with me. This is all the rage up there," she said, twirling around.

"Humph," Jenny growled. "Looks like something for a house of ill repute if you ask me."

"Well, I didn't ask you. I asked Joe and he likes it."

"So be it," Jenny said.

Lillie Mae had bought an enormous rainbow-striped beach umbrella and matching beach blanket with a hole in the middle so the butt of the umbrella could be stuck through and anchored into the white sand. She also had a portable bar with liquors, seltzer bottles, glasses, and a Thermos full of ice cubes. She looked around for Jennings, who was standing behind her in faded, cut-off brown breeches. "Oh, there you are. Please be a dear and carry this heavy old umbrella for us," she said. He took the cumbersome umbrella.

Lillie Mae handed the neatly folded beach blanket to Jenny. "You take this."

Joe came into the room in his new red swim trunks. "Ah, Nina, how wonderful you look!" he said, kissing her on the cheek. "All the men will be so jealous of my good fortune! How can I help you, dear?"

"If you'll take the little bar down, then we can have our drinks by the water."

"Yes, yes. That would be nice," he said, grabbing the straw handle of the portable bar and heading out the screen door.

About that time Lillie Mae called, "Mary Ida, where are you?"

Mother came into the room and nearly fainted at the sight of Lillie Mae. Her face turned beet red when she saw her beautiful older sister prancing about in the scandalous yellow bathing suit, but she didn't say a word.

"There you are, Mary Ida. Will you take the towels?" Lillie Mae said, thrusting a large mound into Mother's hand.

Mother wrapped her arms around the stack of clean towels. "And what are *you* going to take?"

"The lotion," Lillie Mae replied. "Now, is everybody ready? Then let's go."

Truman, Nelle, and I ran ahead of the adults across the hot, sugar-white sand, past the dunes covered in toasty brown sea oats, and down to the green water. It was a calm day with a slight breeze and a slow, rolling surf. Jenny spread the beach blanket on the sand. Daddy opened the huge umbrella, stuck it through the hole, and anchored it in the sand. Joe put the portable bar in a shady spot beneath the umbrella. Lillie Mae and Mother wiped their arms and legs with lotion, then lay down on the blanket beside Daddy, who was stretched out in the sun. Joe and Jenny headed for the water.

After Truman, Nelle, and I swam, we decided to make a sand castle. Finding a place among the dunes, we began to dig. Everywhere around us, little white sand crabs ran sideways up the dunes. We thought it great fun to chase them, even though we were outwitted every time by the feisty crabs, who knew their territory.

"Hey! I have an idea!" Truman exclaimed, out of breath from chasing a crab across two dunes. "Give me your pail, Big Boy."

I handed over my new pail. "See," Truman continued, "the crabs are running up these dunes, then down into this little area. I know how we can catch them." Truman took the pail to a narrow area between two dunes and buried it up to the open top. "We'll let things settle down for a few minutes. Nelle, you go behind that dune and run the crabs up this way. Big Boy, you go over there and do the same thing. I'll stay here and get the crabs behind this dune. When I call *Go*, we'll start the chase."

We scattered, hunched down in the sand, and waited for the signal. Truman called "Go!" Then we started up the dunes, the crabs running ahead of us. The crabs crossed the top of the dunes, ran down the shelf, and plopped into the bucket. Truman jumped up and down. "Ha ha! See! We outwitted them!" Then he hurried down the hill toward the spot where the grown-ups were resting.

Lillie Mae, Mother, and Daddy were dozing. Jenny and Joe were in the water about fifty feet away. Truman found a piece of a newspaper Joe had brought to read and hurried back to Nelle and me.

"Whatcha got?" Nelle asked.

Truman grinned fiendishly. "You want to see some fun?"

We said we did. Truman took the piece of newspaper, carefully folded it across the top of the bucket, and lifted the bucket out of the sand. "Follow me, but be real quiet," he said, holding his finger to his lips.

We walked back to the umbrella. Truman handed me the squirming mass of crabs. Then he stretched out beside Lillie Mae, who was sleeping. Still wearing his beach coat with long sleeves, he flopped over her several times and tried to talk to her. She groaned with sleep-filled eyes barely open and said, "Go and play, Truman." After he wallered and flopped another time or two, he managed to unhook the straps of her bathing suit. Then he got up, reached for the bucket of crabs, spilled them all over the beach blanket, and screamed, "Look out! Crabs! Crabs!"

The crabs ran all over Lillie Mae as they headed for the safety of the dunes. She shrieked and slapped her legs. "Oh! Oh! Get off! Get off!" Dancing about in a fury, she shook so hard that the top of her bathing suit fell to her knees, but she still didn't stop screaming and jumping about. Joe looked up in horror from the water and came running, all the while jabbering in English and Spanish, "Nina, Nina, what is it?" Jenny hurried behind him.

Mother jerked up from her sleep to see Lillie Mae's firm white breasts gyrating in the sunshine. Daddy was too speechless to do anything but gawk. Mother elbowed him in the side to try to make him turn his head. But Daddy wasn't about to shut his eyes.

Nelle and I stood there in disbelief. I'd never seen a grown woman's breasts displayed before. Truman just giggled.

In a matter of a few seconds the crabs disappeared. Then, calmly, as though she were dressing herself in the privacy of her own bedroom, Lillie Mae lifted the front of her bathing suit and fastened the straps. She leaned over, put her arm across my shoulder, and said, "Those sand crabs are awful, aren't they? I'm glad they're gone." I nodded, still feeling embarrassed. She continued, "Isn't that *your* pail?"

*She's blaming this on me,* I thought, looking for Truman, who turned and ran toward the sand dunes. I was so mad I could have punched him in the nose for pulling such a stunt on his mother, then running off and allowing me to take the blame.

"Yes, it's my pail, but I didn't have anything to do with it," I said.

Lillie Mae looked at Truman scampering out of sight behind a sand dune. She patted my shoulder. "It's all right. It was really nothing," she said, smiling with a smile that said, "We'll forgive him, won't we?" Then she turned to Joe. "Why don't you open the bar? I think we could use a drink."

Thinking I'd get a thrashing from Daddy, I could hardly enjoy the rest of our trip to Orange Beach. I was too young to know that Daddy had enough on his mind without correcting me. *He* had to answer to *Mother.* When we got home a day later, Mother and Daddy had a screaming argument over Lillie Mae's scene and Daddy's gaping at her. Mother had some harsh things to say to Daddy ("You always wanted to chase after that hussy! You've had eyes for her since day one! I wouldn't put anything past the two of you!"), which might have been true if he'd had the opportunity. But he never had the opportunity.

# 4

# Captain Wash and the Hen-and-Chickens Succulent

> *[I wanted] to wake up one morning and feel that I was at last a grown-up person, emptied of resentment, vengeful thoughts, and other wasteful, childish emotions. To find myself, in other words, an adult.*
>
> TRUMAN CAPOTE, "Nocturnal Turnings"

*J*enny Faulk's next-door neighbor, Captain Washington Jones, was a proud, stately Civil War veteran over eighty years old, who supported himself and an invalid wife on a three-dollar-a-month veteran's pension. He had lost his sight when some gunpowder blew up in his face during the heat of a battle. Captain Wash, as we children called him, was an imposing giant of a man who wore a knee-length black broadcloth coat and a white shirt with a string tie. His boots were scruffy leather. No one really knew what his face looked like; it was covered by a scraggly gray-and-brown beard that he couldn't see to shave off.

Captain Wash's wife was confined to a wheelchair. The Joneses were always scolding each other in their big old wood house. Mrs. Jones would roll down the long, wide hallway hollering at the Captain, and he'd come along with his cane, tapping about, trying to wait on her. In the summer when the windows were open, practically no conversation was sacred, especially one exchanged in high, angry pitches.

One of Captain Wash's few pleasures and pastimes was coming over to Jenny's house where Callie read the *Montgomery Advertiser* or *Mobile Register* newspaper to him each day. As she read, he'd evaluate the accounts and occasionally burst out with his own assessment of the situation. Conversation was heated at times. The Depression had come to the North, but not to the South. Daily accounts of how the North planned to help the poorer, struggling South seared across the front pages of the newspapers. To a tough old veteran who had lost his sight as well as his beloved Confederate cause, such accounts rang hollow.

Jenny didn't want to hear about it. She came home to have dinner, take off her shoes, and relax for a little while. After all, her millinery business was doing fairly well, and one of the last things she had to worry about was the stock market. She had enough to concern herself with—a house to run and Truman to raise.

Truman had just finished a frustrating first year at school. He thought it beneath his dignity to recite simple letters, words, and sentences when he could recite the alphabet backward and forward and read newspapers. But more than anything else, his difficulty with school lay in his being forced to do something he didn't want to do.

On this particular morning Truman, Nelle, and I sat on the front-porch steps. With our home haircuts, scraped knees, and dirty fingernails, Nelle and I looked like kids ready for summer fun. Truman, with his round face washed clean, and neatly pressed linen shorts and T-shirt, looked like a cherub. But underneath lurked a fiendish imagination. As he was telling Nelle and me how terrible things had been for him in school, he kept looking across the yard beyond the fence at the dirt sidewalk connecting Jenny's house and the other houses up and down the street. Someone had laid boards across the low places in the dirt because these holes filled with water in sudden summer showers. So there was a kind of boardwalk that Captain Wash, Jenny, and the others walked on.

Truman pushed back a strand of blond hair that had fallen on his forehead. "I've been thinking about Captain Wash," he said. "He's about as mean as my teacher. You should have heard him yelling at Mrs. Wash this morning. You heard him, Big Boy. Tell Nelle."

"I heard him," I said. "He called her an old crazy woman. That's what he did. Then he swung his cane like he was going to hit her."

Truman's blue eyes squinted. "He's mean to everybody. He was even mean to me."

"To you?" asked Nelle.

"Sure was. Just the other day when I was sitting with Callie on the sofa as she was about to start reading, Callie asked him, 'Captain Wash, would you mind if Truman read to you today? He's coming along so well in his studies. We're so proud of him.' Then Captain Wash made a face that looked like he'd been sucking green persimmons and he said, 'That pipsqueak! Why he's just a little runt of a boy. I'll not having him read my news.' See, Nelle? See what a mean old man he is? I sure would like to get him. I've been thinking about how to do it."

We knew we could set a clock by Captain Wash. Every day before he came down to the house, he waited for Callie and Jenny to walk by on their way home to dinner. He gave them time to finish eating, then buttoned his black coat, took his cane, and started down his front steps. Using the cane like a big eye, he swept it from side to side, tapping on the furniture, down the steps, along the sidewalk to the fence, and through the iron gate. He had counted the steps along the route from his house to Jenny's gate. He knew, within one or two steps, how many to take. Just like clockwork, Captain Wash arrived every day at twelve-thirty.

"Come in, Captain Wash," Callie would say in her sweet tone.

"Thank you, Miss Callie," he would say, stepping inside, swinging the cane, locating the chair he liked to sit in, and backing against it before easing down.

That's when she would rattle the papers, read the head-lines, and start with the main article. Captain Wash would smile, or grunt, or puff up. Sometimes when he was really interested, he leaned forward, stood his cane on end, then stacked his hands on each other. He seemed to be seeing with his whole body.

"What we'll do," Truman began, "is fix it so Captain Wash can't get here so quick. The old know-it-all ought to be taught a lesson."

"And how'll we do that?" I asked.

"It's easy," said Truman, who told us the plan. We waited in the chinaberry tree house in Nelle's backyard. When Callie and Jenny were safely inside the house, we ran to the front of the house, yanked up the boards in front of Jenny's entrance, and propped them against the gate. Then we hurried inside to eat with everyone else.

"You children are gobbling down your food so fast you'll have the stomachache for sure," Jenny cautioned.

After excusing ourselves from the table, we assembled behind the green leaves of a big wisteria vine near the entrance to the house, and waited. We were just in time, for Captain Wash came tapping along faithfully. He walked exactly the distance to where he should turn in. He stopped, tapped a time or two, paused, and tapped on farther down.

"Don't anybody breathe," Truman whispered.

Captain Wash tapped on down another twenty feet or so before turning around and heading back. Completely disoriented, he reeled.

Truman hopped out from behind the wisteria vine, moved one of the boards propped against the gate, and squeezed through to the sidewalk. He motioned for us to follow.

"Captain Wash, is anything the matter?" Truman asked.

"Where's Miss Callie?" he mumbled, not paying much attention to Truman.

"I'll help you," Truman said, turning the Captain around and heading him across the street toward Dr. Watson's house.

Captain Wash tapped across the road and came to the cement retaining wall around Dr. Watson's house. Confusion was building toward downright anger in the hot summer sun as he hollered, "Somebody in there?"

Dr. Watson came out. He was a huge walrus of a fellow weighing at least three hundred pounds. "Everything all right, Captain? What can I do for you? Let me help you on the porch." He took the elder gentleman's arm and guided him up the steps and onto the porch. Captain Wash was still confused, not knowing where he was.

Hearing voices, Mrs. Watson came outside. She was a prim little woman with gray hair wound in a bun on the back of her head. She thought one of the neighbors might have stopped by to admire her many plants, all potted, pruned, fertilized, and arranged for display on the cement wall around the porch. The enormous pot of tall, forest-green mother-in-law tongue was without equal in Monroe-ville. She had a few dainty cacti resting in yellow and blue ceramic bowls. In the corners, huge long-pronged ferns rested in painted white wicker fern stands. Then there was her pride and joy, the hen-and-chickens succulent, which looked just like a mother hen perched on a pot. The cascading green arms were like little biddies gathered around their mother.

Now everything probably would have turned out all right if we had stayed at Jenny's house and out of sight. But Truman had instigated this adventure and was determined to see it through. So we scampered across the street and crawled on the painted wooden porch.

"Where am I?" Captain Wash asked, trying to steady himself.

Dr. Watson started to answer, but before he could say a word Truman blurted out, "It's like this. Captain Wash started out to get Callie to read to him, but I guess he got turned around. And now . . ."

About that time Captain Wash had zeroed in on where the little voice was coming from, and he'd about come to his senses. With all the fury he could muster, he swung his black cane. Whack! The cane cracked the air. He would have decapitated Truman or anybody else if he could have reached them. Dr. Watson ducked and screamed at his wife, who had already begun to back out of the way.

Captain Wash swung so furiously he nearly reeled himself off the porch. The end of the cane came crashing against the hen-and-chickens succulent. *Crack!* The pot flew off the retaining wall and slammed into the street, breaking into hunks. The little green biddies lay scattered in a dozen places.

Mrs. Watson gasped in horror at the carnage on the other side of the wall.

Nelle and I stood horrified, afraid even to breathe. Truman laughed and clapped his hands with glee. Then we fled back across the street as fast as we could run. We quickly removed the boards against the gate, laid them back over the holes, then hid in the tree house. Fearing what might happen to me when the deed was discovered, I wanted to think of something else besides Mrs. Watson's prized plant lying in smithereens. But not Truman. Immediately he began questioning Nelle and me on the different directions our little adventure might have taken.

"What if Captain Wash had hit me and broken my arm? Would Jenny have taken the gun, run over, and shot him? No, he's a blind old man and that wouldn't have looked too good. As soon as I had fallen on the floor screaming with my arm, then Nelle, you would have run over and told Jenny, grabbed the hoe and given it to her. She would have come over and cut Captain Wash with the hoe.

"Or what if Mrs. Watson had been so mad that she flew into the house, got a pair of scissors and stabbed Captain Wash? No, then she would have had blood all over the porch.

"Another thing that could have happened is that Dr. Watson could have grabbed Captain Wash and wrestled him to the floor. But what if they had rolled down the steps, into the street, and a car had come along?"

Nelle and I were spellbound at all Truman thought of. A few hours passed and nothing was said to us about Captain Wash, and we thought the matter was over with. The after-effects came the next day when Jenny, Callie, Sook, and Bud were on the front porch resting after Sunday dinner. It was a big, pleasant porch with comfortable chairs and Jenny's

plants, among them a prized purple hen-and-chickens succulent in an enormous goblet-shaped pot with grapes down
the sides.

Truman, Nelle, and I came on them sitting quietly and
exchanging small talk: "Is your rheumatism still bothering
your hand, Sook? How is your crop doing this year, Bud?
Is your asthma any better?" Jenny had some sewing in her
lap. Callie was reading a book. Bud was in his rocker, chewing tobacco and spitting in the spittoon. Sook had scissors
to cut out newspaper clippings to paste in her scrapbook.
She had a dip of snuff in her lip and a rag discreetly in her
hand to spit in. She wouldn't publicly use a spittoon, even
if only in the presence of her brother and sisters.

I pulled out my toy fort with cowboys and Indians. Nelle
sat beside me as I set the figures in place. Truman stretched
out on the floor and looked around. He had an uncanny
ability to sense mood. He looked around at the peaceful setting and said, "You all love each other, don't you?"

Jenny, who was nearest him, answered. "Of course we
love each other, Truman. We're kin. We love our kin and
we love you because you're kin, too."

"But don't you have some friends you love better than
you love your kin?"

Bud coughed. The two women squirmed. They remembered Jenny's turbulent affair with the railroad man who
turned out to be married. Then there was Callie's one-sided
love affair with a local doctor. It was Callie who put down
her book and said, "The Bible says blood is thicker than
water, and of course kin is blood."

Truman looked contented because he had managed to bait
the adults out of their peacefulness. Jenny sighed, put down
her sewing, and said, "Where would you be without your

kin? My father raised your great-grandfather, then he raised your grandfather. Then we raised your mother. And now we're raising you."

Truman said, "My mother and father are my kin, but they're not my friends. I had a friend in New Orleans who wanted me. He wanted to keep my mother, too, but Arch wouldn't let him. He used to take mother and me flying in his airplane and that's where I learned to fly."

Truman went over to Nelle and said, "Nelle's my friend. Did you know she saved Big Boy yesterday? Captain Wash was beating him with his cane, and Nelle jumped in and stopped it. Then Dr. Watson stopped Captain Wash from hurting Nelle."

Jenny had a look on her face that as much as said she knew Truman was lying. "And why would Captain Wash have been beating Big Boy?"

Without a pause, Truman said, "Big Boy pushed Mrs. Watson's big nice flower pot with the hens and chicks off the porch. It fell and broke. Come look. You can see where it fell."

The adults looked across the street. Sure enough, the pot had been picked up, but a pile of dirt was still there. "I'll have to see about this tomorrow," Jenny said.

Callie wouldn't let it die. "Big Boy, did you really push Mrs. Watson's pot off the porch?"

Nelle, her back to the adults, leaned over and whispered to me, "Truman's not trying to get you into trouble. He wants to see what will happen."

Jenny jumped into the conversation and saved things for me. "What were you children doing over there on the Watsons' porch anyway?"

Truman must have realized that things were getting out

of hand, so he turned the conversation around. "I'm saying friends are more important than kin, because if my mother was my friend, she would let me come and live with her and I wouldn't have to live with you, my kin."

No one knew what to say. Then Sook stepped in and saved the awkward moment. "Look, Buddy, Big Boy, and Nelle," she said. "See what I put into the scrapbook today. Come help me." She sat on the floor with us and handed Truman the scissors and paper. He started clipping something, but couldn't see for the tears in his eyes.

The next day there was a commotion in the middle of the street. It was Mrs. Watson, so excited that she went out to meet Dr. Watson walking home for dinner. "Can you believe it?" she said. "Sylvester, the colored boy, brought me this huge flowerpot filled with Miss Jenny's purple flowering chicks. I'm the first person to ever get one of her special flowers!"

Dr. Watson said, "I've been telling you all these years Miss Jenny really has a heart of gold. That she was just rough on the outside."

"You've got to do something nice for her," Mrs. Watson continued. "Pull all her teeth for free. Make some new false ones for Miss Sook. Do something!"

I don't know what all took place behind the scenes. I do know that Jenny never said a word about her prized succulent plant and why she had parted with it. It seems that Lizzie, the cook, told Jenny what happened at the Watsons' because she had watched the whole incident from the front window. The end result was that Truman ultimately had his way with Captain Wash, because the old man never did come back for Callie to read to him. And Jenny had to see her hen-and chickens succulent sitting on Mrs. Watson's porch.

# 5
# The Carnival

*I started writing when I was eight—out of the blue, unin-spired by any example. I'd never known anyone who wrote; in fact, I knew few people who read. But the fact was, the only four things that interested me were: reading books, going to the movies, tap dancing, and drawing pictures. Then one day I started writing, not knowing that I had chained myself for life to a novel but merciless master. . . . The most inter-esting writing I did during those days were the plain every-day observations that I recorded in my journal. Long verbatim accounts of overheard conversations. Local gossip. A kind of reporting, a style of "seeing" and "hearing" that would later seriously influence me. . . .*

"Truman Capote by Truman Capote"
*Vogue*, December 1979

*I* suppose Truman and I were the luckiest children in Mon-roeville because one summer we convinced Jenny to build us our own private swimming pool in her side yard. We hadn't started out pestering her about the pool; it just came up kind of naturally. Monroeville had a community pool about a mile down the hill from Jenny's house. Truman, Nelle, and I rode our bicycles down the dusty hill, zigzag-ging around horse-drawn buggies and a few autos to get there. We could swim in the pool anytime we pleased. At least until Sook heard about this young boy, not much older than we were, getting hit by a car while riding his motorcycle through the little town of Peterman, a few miles north of Monroeville. She grieved over that boy even though she didn't know him. Sook got it in her head that we shouldn't be out in the street riding our bikes down to the pool, so she cried to Jenny, "That boy who got killed could have been our Buddy or Big Boy."

Truman picked right up on this. He went on the north side of the house and staked out a pool half the size of Jenny's house. Not wanting to sacrifice any of her japonica bushes or flowers, and knowing that a pool would bring every child in Monroeville to her yard, Jenny wasn't the least bit interested in going through with this project. But after much begging and pleading by Sook, Truman, and me, Jenny softened, then gave in. She convinced her brother-in-law, Frank Salter, to dig the pool.

Anybody would have to know Monroeville's red clay base to realize what a task Frank had ahead of him. Even digging with the sharpest pick, and shoveling until his face turned beet-red in the sun, he could barely make a dent in that cementlike earth. So little by little, the big pool became smaller and smaller, until the final product was only a little larger than a bathtub. When it was finally finished, cemented, and declared ready, we filled it with water from Jenny's flower hose. The neighborhood children flocked over, tracking red clay, leaves, and dirt into the pool when they jumped in, but it was a pool, nonetheless.

Truman assigned Nelle the task of collecting money from anyone other than herself and me who wanted to swim. The children would come up with their nickels, pay Nelle, and she would write down their names in a book. They could leave, go home and return, and if their name was in the book they could swim again.

While Jenny had Frank cornered to dig our pool, she also had him dig a small fish pool on the other side of the house.

She built a little garden around the pool and had a nice shady spot there under the pecan trees and wisteria vines. There weren't any goldfish locally, so she went to Mobile to a pet store to purchase fish for the pool. We kids would gather around the pool and watch the fish grow fat. They'd laze about, swim to the top, open their round mouths, and take food out of our fingers.

We weren't the only ones who enjoyed the fish. Mrs. Ralls's yellow tomcat enjoyed those fish as much as we did. The cat would slip over to the round, shallow pool, hunker down on the side, and try to catch the fish with his paw. What he didn't catch and drag out on the bank he'd injure with his sharp paws. Jenny would see the fish out there dead, floating belly up, and she'd be infuriated. Every time she saw that cat in the yard, she'd run out the back door, grab a handful of rocks, and throw them at the cat as she yelled, "Git from here! I'll blow your head off!"

Every morning at daylight the old cat would slink over from across the street and take his post by the fish pool. One day Jenny had the idea of putting some chicken wire over the pool with wood on it to hold it in place. It was unsightly, but it kept the cat out, even though he'd try to wriggle his paw down through the holes in the wire and grab the fish.

Nelle, Truman, and I watched this cat-and-fish situation with much interest. Truman decided that instead of the cat catching the fish, he'd catch the cat. He lifted one edge of the wire and propped it up with a stick, then tied a string to the stick. Truman, Nelle, and I hid in the bushes early one morning, watching and waiting for the cat. Right on schedule, he came over and prowled around a little bit, eyeing the opening. He stuck his head inside the opening by the stick and squatted on the ledge of the pool. Just as he was leaning over to grab a fish in his paw, Truman jerked the trigger stick, and the wire crashed down over the cat. Truman ran up and quickly put his feet on the wire. He was the only one with shoes on. We gathered around and watched as the old cat became frantic.

The cat was down in the water struggling to get out. He wailed and scratched and pawed at the slime on the sides of the fish pond. Finally he got a hold on the wire and was hanging upside down. He was yowling in fright, and his eyes were as big as silver dollars. Part of him was touching the water, but his head and paws were out. Nelle slipped up with a stick and started punching the cat in the belly to make him turn loose. He fell into the water and tried to swim. Then he managed to climb back up and wrap his paws around the wire. As soon as he did, Nelle punched him back down again. All of us realized the old cat was about to drown, so we took pity on him and let him go. When we lifted the wire, the cat skedaddled out and flew like a blue streak back home. He never came close to the pool again. Even Jenny remarked one day, "I wonder what happened to that old fool tomcat?" The pool got so peaceful she even removed the wire.

I suppose having the fish pool and the swimming pool got us to thinking about fish that morning when we were walking down Drewry Road toward our farm. Some colored folks who were commercial fishermen had rented a house near us, and as we walked by their house that morning, we noticed all the commercial fishing traps and bottle-shaped nets with big hoops, hanging from the trees. The fisherman had dipped the nets in some black preservative and hung them out to drip dry. We saw a group of men hovering around a washtub, talking and pointing at the tub. We hurried up to take a look. It was the strangest-looking fish we'd ever seen. It was some kind of prehistoric catfish. Its jaw jutted out like a swordfish. A colored man named J. C. said the fish was a "sawmouth cat."

Truman was fascinated by the fish. "I'll give you a dollar for him," Truman said. "But part of the deal is that you'll load him up on your truck, tub and all, and bring him to Miss Jenny's house." J. C. was glad to get the dollar and agreed to bring the fish to Jenny's house that afternoon. He just wanted to know if he'd get his tub back. Truman said he wouldn't be needing the tub. After all, he had just the place for the sawmouth catfish—in Jenny's fish pond.

Of course Nelle and I wanted to know what in the world Truman wanted with the catfish, and why he'd dare bring down the wrath of Jenny by putting such a monster in her fish pond, but Truman was as cool as dew on clover. "I have a plan," he said. "We're going to have a sideshow, the likes of which no one has seen in Monroeville, and we're going to make lots of money."

We could hardly wait to get back to town to start planning. That afternoon, J. C. drove up with the fish and dragged the tub around to the side yard. He dumped the fish in the pool. The fish swam around a bit and seemed to be all right. Jenny didn't look in the fish pool, so she didn't know it was there. Then we finished planning what we'd have at our show. We thought of a two-headed chicken. Everybody in Monroeville talked about two-headed chickens, but nobody had ever seen one.

With Sunday dinner coming up, Lizzie, the cook, would be killing chickens. Sook had some big hens fattening in the fattening coop, and she and Lizzie would kill these for chicken pies. Truman found two Rhode Island red hens that looked about the same color. Without asking permission, for he never asked permission for anything but just went ahead and did it, he reached into the coop, picked out a chicken, and started in on Lizzie to kill the chicken.

Lizzie wasn't going to kill and dress chickens until Saturday, but Truman convinced her that he must have the chicken killed that very day. "You can clean her and put her in the ice box," he said. As usual, Truman won his argument. Lizzie didn't kill the chickens by wringing their necks but by chopping off their heads. Truman said, "Let me help, because I need a long neck." We went to the backyard to the cutting post. Lizzie held the hatchet, and Truman stretched the chicken over the post. He pulled the skin on the chicken's neck way back, almost as far as the chicken's shoulders. "Now chop it right there," Truman said. *Klunk!* went the hatchet on the neck. Blood spewed and the chicken flopped.

When Lizzie left to dress the chicken, we were off to continue our scheme. Truman took the chicken's head and inserted a clothes-hanger wire into the severed neck. Then we took one of the live red hens and wired the neck around and under her feathers. The second head stuck off to an angle. I hurried inside the house and got some model airplane glue and glued some of the feathers down smooth. Nelle took a needle and thread and sewed the eyes open on the dead chicken's head.

We stood back to admire our work, but the chicken was out to destroy it. She took her foot and tried to scratch off the appendage. She even broke the glue loose a time or two. "Tie its legs together," Truman said.

"No," Nelle said, grabbing up the chicken. Before we knew what was happening, she put the chicken's right leg on the chopping block, grabbed a brick, and smashed the chicken's toes. "It won't try to scratch the head off now," she said. The chicken limped a little, but it didn't try to scratch.

We moved the big washtubs out of the wash shed. There was a bench under the eaves of the shed, and we moved it into the shed to hold our displays. We put the two-headed chicken in one of Sook's chicken coops and placed it on the bench. We even convinced Sook to make up a display. Sook had a few sacred things once belonging to her father, William Jasper Faulk, a Civil War veteran. She carefully took out the relics. There was a sword and a pistol, a .36-caliber Colt he'd liberated from a Yankee soldier. There was a small French pistol and a tattered gray uniform jacket with gold braid on the collar. William Jasper had survived a battle after all the officers in his regiment were killed, and he was commissioned a second lieutenant in the field. Sook took a large framed picture of William Jasper, folded the uniform coat around it, and arranged it just right under the face so it looked as though he was wearing the coat. She placed the belt and sword on the coat, along with a thin brass buckle with the letters CSA—Confederate States of America. There was a notch or so on the sword, and Truman said, "That stands for the Yankees he killed."

We thought and thought of another display. The one thing that we knew for certain fascinated all the children was unborn babies. Truman had seen a pickled animal fetus, a pig or a sheep, in a jar at Dr. Hines's office. Dr. Hines was a practicing veterinarian not far from Jenny's house. "I'll see if Dr. Hines will loan us the jar and we'll display it as a real baby," Truman said. Sure enough, Truman talked Dr. Hines into letting us borrow the fetus.

When we checked on our catfish in Jenny's fish pool, it was dead, floating belly up. "I can fix it," Truman said. He pulled up the washtub, put sand in the bottom, then filled the tub with water. Then he took a straightened clothes hanger, ran it through the catfish from its mouth to its tail, tied it to a brick, and buried the brick in the sand. So now the catfish was on the sand, looking very much alive. When Truman talked about the fish, he moved the water with his hand, and this slight wave action made the fish move.

Truman decided that we needed a hula dancer to attract people and get them in. "Hula for us, Nelle," he said. Nelle twisted around a bit, but she was stiff as a stick and would never pass the grade as a hula dancer. Then Truman thought of our aunt Lucille, who had just graduated from high school. She was an attractive girl with soft brown hair, nice skin, and a shapely body, but about as deaf as a post.

The next thing we needed was some music. Truman said we would get Anna Stabler, who lived behind the Lees' house, to provide some music for the hula dancing. Though she wasn't much to look at, Anna could play the guitar and banjo. With her long black hair and dark skin, she tried to pretend that she was an Indian. If there was any Indian blood in her it came from somewhere on her mother's side, because her mother was a Negro woman and her daddy was a white judge. Though her daddy wouldn't claim her in his own home, he did not want her living among the other coloreds in the quarters. So he set her up in this little shack behind the Lees' house, in the best neighborhood in town. Anna was a notorious bootlegger who liked to drink, and sometimes when she got drunk she walked right up to the front door of her daddy's house and demanded to see him. He'd come to the door and visit with her for a while. Then she was content to return home.

Truman, Nelle, and I went to see Anna to tell her about our sideshow. She said she could play hula music and would come to the show. Now all we had to do was get everything ready. We put our displays on the wash shelf and separated them with old boards. Truman rolled out two barrels that held Sook's chicken corn and turned these over. Then we helped him drag out an old door from beneath the barn. He put the door on top of the barrels, and this was to be the stage for Lucille's hula dance. We brought Sook's rocker from the back porch. Anna was to sit in the rocker and strum her guitar. We took some old boards and rigged up an entrance that people would have to pass through. This was so that Truman could collect their nickel as they went in to see the displays.

Lucille wanted to know what to wear. "Get a croker sack and cut thin strips in it so it will look like the grass of a hula skirt," said Truman. "And put on a short top."

When Lucille returned for the show, our eyes nearly popped out. She'd gotten her mother, our cousin Abby, whom we called Cuddin Abby, to help Lucille fix a costume worthy of the afternoon entertainment. Lucille wore a hula skirt made of a croker sack, but the strips were hemmed neatly so they looked like slender strings. She wore skimpy briefs underneath. She had on a bright-colored top that looked like a bra, so her midriff was exposed. Cuddin Abby also made bracelets for Lucille's feet and wrists and braided flowers in her hair.

At two o'clock that afternoon, Anna appeared, wearing a bright yellow blouse that pulled down off the shoulders, and voluminous white slips. She'd hidden a pint of whiskey in her slips, and we could tell by the way her breath smelled that she'd already been sampling from the bottle. Truman hummed a Hawaiian tune and asked Anna if she could play that. Anna took a seat in the rocking chair, strummed her guitar, and began to wail "Birmingham jail house, Birmingham jail," a tune she'd heard at a roadhouse. Lucille couldn't hear the music. She thought Anna was playing some kind of Hawaiian tune, so she began to shimmy and twist in a hula dance.

It didn't take very long for a crowd of children to gather, fork over their nickels, and *oooh* and *ahhh* at the displays. They marveled at the two-headed chicken, the prehistoric catfish, and the real baby fetus in a jar. Anna pulled her slips up to her face, uncapped the bottle, and swigged on the whiskey all afternoon. She was soon pie-eyed. Lucille danced her heart out, even working up a sweat. We had a great show.

It should have ended there, and if it had, then we and Jenny would have been spared the terrible embarrassment of the following day. But we were exhausted when the afternoon was over; we didn't take time to dismantle the displays and put the wash house back in order. All I remember is eating a biscuit and jam, drinking some milk, and falling to sleep about the time darkness came.

The next day was Sunday. Sook called for Truman and me to get up, wash, and dress to go to Sunday school with Jenny and Callie. At ten o'clock we had to be dressed and walking to church. After Sunday school, Truman and I hurried back home and into the kitchen to see Sook's chicken pie. This Sunday the pie was only halfway up the pan, so we figured there wouldn't be a big crowd for dinner. Sook gave each of us a kiss on the top of our head and said, "You boys don't get dirty, now. The preacher, his missus, and Sonny will be here to eat with us. Won't that be nice?"

Our faces fell. We hated Sonny Blake. He was the most disgusting boy we knew, even if he was the preacher's son.

Not only was he a big bully, but he had bored a hole in the wall to the girls' bathroom. Somebody had caught him masturbating while he looked through the hole in the wall at the girls. We thought this was about the crudest, most uncouth thing we could think of. And we weren't the only ones who thought it. All the boys we knew thought Sonny was loony for doing something that dumb. The very last thing Truman and I wanted to do was sit at the same table with him.

But before we could hatch some scheme to take us away, the Blakes were ringing Jenny's doorbell. "Now you boys be nice to Sonny," Sook said, taking the huge pan of chicken pie to the dining-room table. Even though the table was set with Jenny's finest Bavarian china and sterling silver, the one dish that was always served in the container it was cooked in was Sook's pie.

We all sat around the table. Preacher Blake said a short prayer before the meal; he'd learned not to pray a sermon at Jenny's table. If he did, Jenny would squirm and clack the silver. Everyone at the table served themselves as the big dish of chicken pie made the rounds. Jenny was in good humor that day, witty, talking about some amusing incidents that happened at the store and some interesting things she'd seen on her buying trips to other cities.

Everything was tolerable, even our slight conversation with Sonny, until Lucille opened her big mouth. "Oh, Preacher Blake, you should have seen our wonderful sideshow yesterday. Children and grown-ups came from all over town just to see the displays and have fun."

The preacher seemed interested in what she had to say. "And when are you going to have another performance?"

Then Jenny chimed in. "Why, they could stage it again for you after dinner. A command performance."

Truman and I looked at each other and groaned. Jenny

excused us from the table with orders to round everybody up for a special performance. She said the grown-ups and Sonny would wait on the front porch until everything was ready. Lucille hurriedly put on her Hawaiian costume; I ran for Nelle and told her to get Anna. When Anna arrived she was hung over. Her hair wasn't combed. She had blobs of red rouge on her cheeks. She had one cheek puffed out with the cotton, but the other cheek was sunken in. With her banjo in hand, she sat down in Sook's rocking chair. Truman, Nelle, and I checked the exhibits. The old chicken was still alive, although the extra head was wilted and drawing flies. The fish seemed to be doing all right and didn't stink too badly.

Truman announced, "It's time to begin!" Anna took a swig of whiskey and started playing "Birmingham Jail House." Seeing her strumming, Lucille thought the hula music had begun, so she crawled onto the wooden door and began undulating and moving her hands. As the preacher, his wife, and Sonny started to enter the wash house, Truman stopped them and demanded their nickels. The preacher screwed up his mouth sort of disgusted-like, fished around in his blue suit pants for some change, and handed Truman fifteen cents. The music also attracted the attention of the neighborhood children, who had put on their swimsuits and jumped into the pool. One little boy had a black inner tube wedged around his middle.

Preacher Blake could hardly keep his eyes ahead for looking over at Lucille's gyrating back end. He'd take a few steps, then his head would swivel back to see her bare midriff, her white legs, and her swinging hips. Sonny was the same way. He was trying to get close enough to her to look under her skirt. The preacher didn't seem to show any interest in the two-headed chicken, the fish, the Confederate display, or even the baby fetus. He was straining his eyeballs out to get a good look at Lucille.

About that time Mrs. Blake shrieked and clutched her throat. "Oh, my God! They've got a baby! Whose baby is that?" She was screaming and carrying on, not that we had the thing, but over whose baby it was, like she wouldn't have anything to tell if she didn't know whose baby was pickled in formaldehyde. Truman tried to quiet her by giving some spiel about the display, but she wasn't listening. She tugged on her husband and finally got his eyes jerked back from Lucille. He looked at the pig fetus and he screamed. The kids gathered around, and then the bench holding the displays teetered and fell to the ground. The fetus smashed and rolled out at Mrs. Blake's feet. She screamed her loudest and nearly fainted. Then they all fled backward out of the wash house.

In their mad rush to get out, the crowd knocked the door off the drums, and Lucille fell forward over some of the smaller children. She was hanging there with her back end up in the air. Preacher Blake tried to help Lucille, but the part he was reaching for was up in the air. In the crush to move along, the preacher, Mrs. Blake, Sonny, and some of the other children stumbled and fell into the swimming pool. The two-headed chicken flopped up the edge of the driveway. Sonny saw it, scrambled out of the pool, and made a mad dash for it. "Grab the chicken! It's a two-headed chicken!" he screeched, running down the road.

Truman, Nelle, and I stood around wondering how in the world things had gone to hell in a flash. We started over to help the Blakes out of the pool when we heard pistol shots out in the road. We forgot about the Blakes and darted into

Jenny's front yard in time to see Sheriff Farrish standing on a cement retaining wall in front of his house. He was holding a smoking pistol in his hand. By this time everybody in the neighborhood had gathered around and was looking up at the red-faced sheriff, who said, "A two-headed chicken was running down the road. Did anybody see it? I think I shot off one of its heads, but it kept on running."

The neighbors shook their heads and mumbled, "Drinking on a Sunday afternoon. Mmmm. Mmmm. For shame. And shooting a pistol right here in the middle of town! Nearly killed the preacher's boy. Ain't no telling who he'd kill if he had the chance."

About this time Preacher Blake and his skinny wife pulled themselves out of the pool and were out in the street with all the others. Now Mrs. Blake couldn't really see what she looked like with her wet clothes all clinging to her body like gauze around a mummy. Underneath she had more ridges, bumps, buckles, straps, and lines than anybody had ever seen. Even Jenny clenched her teeth to keep from bursting out laughing as the Blakes stomped off down the street on their way home. Nobody uttered a word as Mrs. Blake tried to maintain her dignity and pull away the dress plastered to her skin. In the background, Anna Stabler hadn't missed a wailing line of "Birmingham Jail House."

Truman, Nelle, and I scampered for the safety of the tree house to discuss the events of the day, and for Truman to record them in one of his little notebooks. Although everything wasn't completely our fault, we figured we'd get blamed for it anyway, and maybe if we hid out, the worst would blow over. We managed to salvage our jar of nickels and stash it in the tree house for special treats.

We fell on the floor laughing over Mrs. Blake's reaction

to the pig fetus and the way she looked all wet and scraggly. I don't think she ever lived down or explained what she had on under her dress that day. From that time on, anytime I saw her she was in a voluminous dress with great folds and pleats, and there wasn't any way that anything could stick to her. The Blakes soon left town, taking Sonny with them.

When the election rolled around that fall, Sheriff Farrish was defeated. Lucille headed off to college, but not before deciding she needed a hearing aid.

As for the two-headed chicken, we never saw her again. I guess she's still running through the woods with pistol balls ringing in her ears.

# 6

# The Trimotor Ford

> *Then there was that awful, frightened moment when I knew*
> *it was just a dream, and the plane would sit there on the*
> *ground. Pretty soon everyone else realized it, too, but only a*
> *few of them got mad. The rest were only sorry and sad in*
> *the way that I was sorry and sad: here was simply more*
> *proof that the world is not a magic place and that we must*
> *expect no magic from it.*
>
> PM's *Picture News*, in
> *Truman Capote: Conversations*

*If* Nelle and I ever coveted anything, it was Truman's green
Trimotor Ford airplane. We had never seen anything like it.
In those first years after Lindbergh crossed the Atlantic, people were infatuated with airplanes and the whole idea of flying. Monroeville, Alabama, was quite isolated back then, so
we had to drive to Greenville, a little town about thirty miles
away, to catch the train. Although train rides were common,
I don't suppose anybody in our town had flown, except
maybe Truman and his mother, Lillie Mae.

Truman told several tales about how he acquired this
child-size Trimotor Ford plane built like a tricycle with two
front wheels and one rear wheel. One of his explanations
was that some men from the Monroeville lumber mill pitched
in and bought the plane for him out of gratitude because he
drew their portraits or penned some poems for them.

Later in life he wrote a short story, "One Christmas,"
about visiting his father in New Orleans and convincing him

to buy the plane for his special Christmas present. Neither version is correct. Truman did get the plane in New Orleans, however, because he brought it back with him on the train when he and Lillie Mae returned from a visit to see Arch. I went to Greenville with Jenny Faulk to meet their train, and there was Truman grinning and pointing to the men who were unloading it.

It is unlikely that Truman got the plane from either of his parents. Those were hard times for Lillie Mae. She was divorcing Arch, had little money, and was certainly not able to afford any such toy as the Trimotor Ford. Arch was poor, so he didn't have any money, either. The story Truman told Nelle and me was that he "won it by guessing the number of jelly beans in the terminal building at the New Orleans airport."

Some of the airlines servicing New Orleans in those days flew Trimotor Fords. Truman said one company, as a promotion, put a big jar of jelly beans in the airport lobby, and the person who correctly guessed the number of beans in the jar won a prize. One prize was a muskrat coat, another was a shotgun, and another was the Trimotor Ford airplane.

There is no question that Truman had been inside the airport, for he described it in detail the same way I saw it years later. "The airport is so big, with planes buzzing all about," he said. "There is a rose compass in the tile floor. On the walls are scenes of foreign places I'm going to visit one day. And there's a big globe in one corner."

That particular day when we arrived back in Monroeville after getting Truman, Lillie Mae, and the plane, Nelle was waiting for us on Jenny's porch. She and I begged Truman to let us ride in the plane, which he refused to do. Later, he gave us short, stingy rides and then insisted that we get out.

Green with envy, we begged him to tell us how he got it. He said he and Lillie Mae had flown to Tuscaloosa to see his grandmother, leaving Arch behind because Arch was afraid to fly (which wasn't true, because in later years I flew Arch plenty of places). Truman said right after he and Lillie Mae took off and headed north, the pilot, dressed in a dark blue uniform with silver stripes on his coat cuffs, came back to see the passengers. Lillie Mae was scared, and the pilot put his arm around her to comfort her. He was a very handsome pilot with dark, curly hair, a tiny pencil-line mustache, and straight white teeth.

Truman said Lillie Mae cried and said, "My little Truman wishes he could learn more about airplanes. Would you show him?" The end result, according to Truman, was that the pilot took him to the cockpit and let him fly the plane. As Truman flew toward Tuscaloosa, he saw a huge cloud ahead. All of a sudden lightning flashed. Truman grabbed the plane's wooden control wheel, wrenched it to the left, banked the plane vertically, and whizzed past the lightning. His quick action saved the plane and its passengers.

The pilot congratulated him on his bravery and thought everything was so wonderful that he'd do something special for Truman. The pilot just happened to have a friend who had counted the jelly beans as they went into the jar at the terminal. The pilot whispered the number to Truman. Then, when they returned to the New Orleans airport, Truman named the number and claimed the prize.

Truman told Nelle and me the plane was his award for valor. We had no reason to doubt it one way or the other. That was secondary. Our primary interest was in figuring out some way to convince him to let us ride in it. He'd play with it, pedaling up and down Jenny's wide hall, or taking it outside on the walk and pedaling it up and down between the porch steps and the front gate. When Truman tired of playing in the plane, he took it back to Sook and Jenny's bedroom (he was sleeping in the double bed with Sook at that time). There were two double beds in the room. Jenny's was nearer the door and Sook's nearer the window. Truman wedged his plane between Sook's bed and the wall. If he was away for a few hours, he'd run back to her room to check and make sure the plane was exactly as he had parked it.

Nelle and I seized every opportunity to drag the plane out and pedal it up and down the hall. Then we'd hurry to put it back before Truman caught us. On this particular day, Lillie Mae took Truman away for a few days to visit friends. If Truman hadn't been so stingy about the plane, then I suppose we wouldn't have been so anxious to be sneaky and daring. For once I wish we'd left well enough alone.

With Lillie Mae and Truman away visiting, and Jenny and Callie at the store, Nelle and I saw how to make our move. We knew Lizzie, the cook, would tidy up and leave for home after noonday dinner, and that would leave only Sook at home. She would take a drink of her medicine right after eating, then lie down and sleep for an hour or so. Nelle and I heard Sook twist open the brown glass quart jar that she kept on a shelf in her closet. Peeking through the crack in the door, we saw her take the tablespoon by the side of the jar, fill the spoon with rheumatism medicine, turn the spoon up to her mouth, grimace at the taste, then put the spoon and jar back on the shelf. Then she stretched across the bed and closed her eyes.

"Sook'll be asleep in a minute," I said.

"Then what'll we do?" said Nelle.

"We'll slip in as quiet as mice, pull out the plane, and play as long as we want to."

"Pull out the plane! Oh, Big Boy!" Nelle said in a voice just loud enough that Sook stirred on the bed.

"Now look what you've done. You woke her," I said.

We waited a minute while Sook drifted back to sleep. Nelle whispered, "No I didn't. She's asleep now."

"Well, we're gonna let her get good asleep."

We waited a few minutes longer, then tiptoed in beside the bed, eased the plane out, and pushed it down the hall. We carefully opened the front door and pulled the plane down the steps, across the yard, and onto the sidewalk. Nelle played stewardess awhile, and I was the pilot. Then it was Nelle's turn to be the pilot and I played gunner.

After tiring of going up and down the sidewalk, we thought of other things we could do with the plane. I had the idea of taking Jenny's empty wooden cloth frames she had brought home from her store and attaching these to the plane. These three-foot-long frames were covered in light-weight paper. Nelle and I pushed the plane to the barn, where we found Jenny's tools. We nailed the frames to two-by-fours and wired one on the back of the plane for a stabilizer.

"I know it'll fly," I insisted, "if we can get up enough speed." I looked up at the sloping roof. "If we can get it up there, we can fly it off the roof and land it on Mr. Jones's grass yard easy as pie."

We found Jenny's wooden ladder and set it upright. Then I pulled and Nelle pushed the plane up the ladder until we reached the top of the tin-roofed barn. It was a warm summer day, and sweat rolled off our bare backs. But I'd forgotten something very important—my dime-store goggles and black oilcloth pilot's helmet. I hurried back into the house, found the helmet and goggles, then climbed back up the ladder and into the cockpit.

I put on the goggles and snapped the chin strap in place. "Nelle, I want you to push me with all your might."

"Okay," she said. "But Big Boy, we better do this right."

"Why do ya say that?"

"Well, look down there. Mr. Jones's hog waller is right below us. And those two big old hogs are down in it somewhere."

"Oh, don't worry about that. I'm going to fly *over* the hog pen and the fence and glide down on the grassy spot. You'll see."

Nelle grabbed hold of the rear of the plane. "Are you ready?"

"I'm ready," I said. "Now I'll stick my hand up, and when I drop it down, you shove hard."

"Okay. You'll be flying by the time you get to the edge of the barn," she said.

I knew I'd better aim for the grassy spot, not climb out and risk stalling the plane. I worked it out in my mind. Then I dropped my hand.

"Pedal, Big Boy! Pedal!" Nelle screamed as she gave the plane a tremendous shove.

Everything was under control. The Trimotor Ford sailed off the edge of the barn. *I was flying!* Then all of a sudden, instead of gliding over the pigpen and fence and landing on the grassy spot, the plane started to drop. *Bloop!* Holding on for dear life, I still hadn't lost control. There were two big hogs lying in the pond. One had heard the racket of the plane rattling down the topside of the tin roof, and she raised her head out of the water just in time to see the plane ram her side with a big *Whomp!* She'd never walk straight again.

The other old hog was excited, too, and as she stood up in shock, the plane careened off the first hog and hit her head-on. I sailed out of the plane into the water, and the plane went under the hog. Mud, trash, and manure slopped everywhere. I struggled to get my goggles off. One old hog had the plane hung in her leg. She kicked and thrashed and struggled to drag herself to higher ground.

About that time Nelle screamed, "The hogs'll get you and eat you alive!" I turned and looked up to see her hold her nose and leap off the barn. She splashed down, sending a wave of nasty, muddy water over the two of us as she landed atop one of the detached, floating wings. We blubbered and sputtered. Nelle grabbed my arm. "Hurry! You gotta get out! *We* gotta get out," she yelled.

The hogs fled out of the slop hole. The one that had been dragging the plane kicked it off. That's when Nelle and I grabbed the smashed plane and heaved it across the fence. Then we crawled over to safety.

"Are you okay?" Nelle asked, looking at my mud-covered body.

"I'm okay. What about you? Look at your hair!"

"I don't want to see it," Nelle said. "I don't think anything's broken," she added, shaking her arms and legs.

Then we looked at the plane. "Oh, no. What are we going to do, Big Boy?"

"We've got to get the plane away from here," I said. There was no opening in Jenny's fence, so we either had to go around the front of the Joneses' house, down the main highway, and back up Jenny's front walk, or go through the Mimses' pasture at the back of the house. We decided on the pasture route. We dragged the plane back to Jenny's barn, hooked up the water hose, and washed the mud and manure off each other from head to toe. We looked over the plane, all muddied, scrunched up, and hog-stomped. "It'll never fly again," I said, realizing that what the crash hadn't done the hog had finished.

"What'll Truman say?" Nelle said. "He'll be back tomorrow and he'll kill us for sure if he finds out what we've done. That doesn't give us much time to figure something out."

"Let's clean it up as good as we can," I said, "then take it back and put it where we found it. We'll think of something."

We hosed down the broken plane and silently dragged it up the steps and down the hall. Sook was still sleeping peacefully, so we put it over by her bed. Only this time, without its sturdy propeller and stubby wings, it slid easily into place.

Nelle looked sad about the whole thing. "Now what'll we do?"

"Let me think," I said. We sat on the front porch steps to talk. I knew I couldn't tell Sook a lie if she came right out and asked me what happened to the plane. "I'm not sure if we told Truman the truth if he'd believe us—or ever forgive us," I said.

"Oh, Big Boy, I hate this. I hate what we did."

About that time, a beat-up old pickup truck rounded the corner in a cloud of dust and roared off down the road. I had an idea. "I think I know how we can get out of it. We'll tell them *some* of the truth. We'll say we broke all the rules by taking the plane out without asking Truman. Then we'll say we got thirsty and left it by the curb when we went inside to get a drink of water. Yes! That's what we'll say. And then we can blame it on Uncle Howard."

"Why your Uncle Howard?"

" 'Cause Uncle Howard's usually drunk and drives his big old pickup truck like something gone crazy. Like that fool man that just passed by. We'll hint that it was probably Uncle Howard that ran into it at the curb."

"Yeah," Nelle said. "Uncle Howard did it. Poor Uncle Howard."

"Poor us, 'cause now we don't have the plane to play with anymore," I said. "And if the truth ever gets out, we're goners for sure. So cross your heart and hope to die you'll never tell." Then we hurried home to safety.

I stayed away from Jenny's house almost a week. When I finally found the nerve to face Truman, I saw the remains of the smashed plane lying on the trash heap, ready to be picked up and hauled away by the garbage collector. Truman met me at the front gate and was the first to speak. "Nelle said Uncle Howard probably ran over my plane."

"I'm real sorry, Truman. Nelle and I are sorry we took it out and let something bad happen to it."

"I'm glad you weren't here to see me cry, Big Boy," Truman said. "I cried hard over my plane. I really liked that plane, probably more than anything in the world. I wish I was a magic person, then I'd fix it back. I'd make a lot of things right again. But then I guess there's no such thing as magic anymore."

# 7
# Popguns, Rubber Guns, and Jenny

*I've never lived by other people's values.*

"An Interview with Truman Capote,"
*McCall*'s, November 1967

$T$ruman and Jenny had a rather unusual relationship. Jenny, who was born in 1873, was in her late fifties when Lillie Mae brought Truman to live with her. My mother, Mary Ida, said Lillie Mae and Jenny were always at odds about something while Lillie Mae was growing up, but Truman never openly crossed horns with Jenny in an argument. I don't think he liked her, but he respected her. He was even a little bit afraid of her.

Truman had his own way of disobeying Jenny. She would ask him to do things in the house, and invariably he'd mess up what he was supposed to do. If he was to carry something, he'd spill it. Or if he was to move something for her, he'd knock it over. If she wanted him to water her flowers, he'd stick the hose in the ground, gouge up holes, and flood the yard. He reasoned that after a time she'd quit asking him to do things. It must have worked, because, for the most part, they had a live-and-let-live relationship. Jenny let Truman go his own way, and in return he didn't aggravate her. But one day Truman pushed Jenny too far, and she let him have it. And since he was one to harbor grudges, he waited for the opportune moment to strike back.

The vendetta began with a popgun. Now these weren't just ordinary popguns. They were made from a straight-growing, long-stemmed bush that grew wild. The stem had a pithy core, which was scraped out with a piece of metal. The gun part was about fifteen inches long and, when scraped clean, looked very much like a clean-bored gun barrel. The rammer was a piece of hardwood whittled to slip down into the bore. This was used to pump up the gun and fire the chinaberries.

A green chinaberry has pulp around a hard center seed. This pulp acts like a gasket when the chinaberry is squeezed into a popgun barrel. We would load one chinaberry into the popgun. Then we'd rotate the popgun and start another berry in at the other end. As we pushed the berry with the hardwood stick rammer, air would compress in the gun. The chinaberry in the end would pop out like a shot out of a shotgun. *POP!* It would shoot a long distance and sting like fire when it hit.

George, a field hand who worked for my Daddy, made my popgun. Truman and Nelle's guns were made by John White. In the summer it was great sport to have chinaberry fights. When Jenny was away at the store, we'd get carried away. Sometimes we'd do the forbidden—run down the great hall at Jenny's house, shooting and yelling at one another. Jenny had a big bookcase in the hall, and we'd hide beside it and ambush one another. One day Nelle was cornered there squealing and hollering because Truman and I were popping our guns at her. She wasn't really crying, but we had stung her a time or two, and she felt like we had the best of her.

About the time all this was going on, Jenny came in from the store, heard all the commotion, and rushed over to Truman and me. She grabbed our guns and said, "I'll stop this right now! There's no sense in hurting a girl."

Truman's gun was empty. My gun had just been loaded and had the plunger in. Truman, who played in neat linen shorts, had bent over Nelle, and his round little bottom was sticking up in the air. Before we knew what had happened, Jenny rammed the plunger of my gun with her hip and *BAM!* the chinaberry hit Truman right in the seat. He let out a shriek. "Sook! Sook! Jenny shot me with the popgun!" When Sook came to see about Truman, he ran to her for comfort.

Sook grabbed him up in her arms. She gave Jenny a stern look. "Jenny, what are you doing? You've got Truman squawling. Nelle's squawling. What's going on in here?"

Jenny acted all apologetic, saying she "couldn't understand why that thing went off."

"Come on, children. Come on in the kitchen with me," Sook said, still holding him tightly. We left Jenny in the hall picking up chinaberries and followed Sook into the kitchen. There she wiped Truman's tears with a wet dishcloth and soothed his hurt pride. Then we sat down and ate tea-cake cookies dipped in coffee.

Now that our popguns were confiscated, we had to look for something else to do. We decided if we couldn't play with popguns, we'd make some rubber guns from pieces of wood with a handle and long barrel sawed out. We searched everybody's house, woodshed, and garage for the right-sized wood or plank. Then we used Jenny's tools from her shed to cut a two-foot-long barrel. We took a wooden clothes-pin, lashed it to the pistol grip, and attached a strong rubber band to the top of the clothespin. Our rubber bands were made from discarded inner tubes that we found by combing Monroeville's trash piles, particularly at the filling stations. We always tried to keep extra ammunition stashed away, but our supplies were running low. The rubber bands were three-quarters of an inch wide, stretching from the end of the pistol barrel to the clothespin. We'd point to what we wanted to shoot, press the rear end of the clothespin, and the band would fly out with a *WHACK!*

We'd spend hours at a time chasing around Jenny's ja-ponica bushes, shooting at one another. Our main inspira-tion was a cowboy adventure story that we saw every Saturday at the picture show. Our cowboy heroes swung first, shot first, never kissed the girls, and had great affection for their pistols. We had great affection for *our* pistols—we sanded, scraped, and polished them until they glistened.

One day Truman came out to play holding the most beautiful rubber gun I ever saw. The barrel top was notched out like castle embankments so he could load several rubber bands at one time. The wood was stained dark walnut. It was whittled to fit his hand just right. Nelle and I begged him to tell us where he got it, but he just grinned and said, "I made it." We doubted him. But we didn't have to wait long, for the truth finally came out one Sunday.

Usually after church the family assembled on the porch or in the living room at Jenny's house. This particular Sun-day we gathered in the living room because Mother was going to play the piano. Jenny had big horsehair sofas and chairs and plenty of room for guests. Frank and Mary Sal-ter (Jenny's sister and brother-in-law) were there, as were Mother and Daddy, Sook, and Jenny. Truman came in with

Nelle and me. Nelle and I had checked our rubber guns in the hall before we came in, because we knew if Jenny saw them she'd take them. "To protect my vases," she'd say. Truman had stuffed his in his back pocket.

We were all waiting for the piano playing to begin when Frank looked at Truman and said, "Did the piece fit that I made for you?"

Truman nodded silently and got up to leave. Frank had Nelle's and my attention immediately. He got Jenny's attention, too, because she asked, "What was it that Truman needed?"

Frank looked for all the world like he wished he'd never opened his mouth, but there was nothing left to do but explain. "Truman said he accidentally broke the side off one of your tables and he asked me to make a piece to fit it." Frank drew in the air and said it was "shaped like this, with a long, protruding part, notched out, and shaped sort of like a . . ." His voice trailed off as he realized that he was about to say "like a pistol grip." The table that Truman had described as being broken was sitting right there in the living room. Frank could see that nothing was broken. His voice came to a quiet halt.

Meanwhile, Nelle reached behind Truman's back and yanked out his rubber gun. She held it up and said, "Is *this* the piece you made for the broken table?" Frank looked startled, but didn't say anything. We could tell by the look on his face that he'd made the piece, and that he'd been conned into making a very nice rubber gun.

With all the adults sitting there looking first at Frank, then at Truman, I thought Truman would have been mortified. There he was, caught in the act, and his face wasn't even red. When Truman realized all eyes were on him like they expected an explanation, he turned and began a soft-shoe tap-dance routine. He slid his feet and danced, tipped an imaginary hat, and turned around. He tap-danced to the hall door, stepped out, and bowed. Everybody was so dumbfounded by the performance that they applauded, then went immediately into a conversation, saying, "That kind of talent ought to be in vaudeville."

Jenny said, "My goodness, I never saw anything that good at a Chautauqua!"

With Truman out the door and the grown-ups distracted from the original thought about the gun, Nelle and I slipped away, too, grabbing our guns on the way out. I thought Truman would have lit into Nelle, but he didn't. He was too busy thinking of how we were going to get more ammunition.

Now Jenny had a new four-door automobile in the barn parked where Sook used to keep the horse and buggy. When the horse died, Jenny got rid of the buggy. She renovated the barn by having two strips of cement put down to drive the car on. During the week, the car stayed in the barn. But come Sunday afternoon, Jenny liked to go to the cemetery or visit her friends. Since she couldn't drive, she relied on my daddy to drive her and my mother on their "calling" rounds.

It was a production to get the car ready, even for a short trip. Daddy would have to check under the hood, crank and warm up the engine, then back out. Above all, he had to check and make sure the spare tire was ready for an emergency. There were only dirt roads back then, and people expected to have a flat when they went for a drive. Looking for excitement, little kids who lived along the dirt road would embed nails in the dirt and in the ruts so cars would have flats. It gave the kids something to do to stand around and watch the people laboring to change a tire. The tire had to be dismantled, the tube pulled out, patched, and stuffed back into the tire. Then the tube had to be pumped back up with a hand pump. It took quite a lot of work and a lot of time to fix a flat. Jenny was aware of this, too, so she kept a new spare for her car.

At Jenny's barn there was a small drop-off from the end of the cement strips to the ground. Daddy always laid a board across the drop-off so there wouldn't be a bump when he backed out. That afternoon, Truman took long nails and stuck them in the crack where the board jutted against the cement runners. Sure enough, when Daddy backed the car out and rolled over the crack, a nail punctured the right rear tire. We could hear the hissing and whizzing as air escaped and the tire started going flat. Truman ran around and gathered up the other nails and hid them. Daddy had on his good clothes, so he fussed and grumbled as he set about changing the tire. He had to chock the wheels, jack up the car, remove the deflated tire, and put on the spare. Jenny insisted that Daddy patch the tire as well, because she didn't want to go off without a spare.

In one of the few scenes in which I saw Daddy bow his back to Jenny, he said, "I'm in my Sunday clothes, and I'm *not* going to patch the tire. It can wait until Monday."

Jenny had a fit. She was ready to go. "Well, *I'll* get the tire fixed!" she said, slamming the door behind her and stomping back into the house. She called up Johnny Wiggins, a garage owner who was at home on Sunday afternoon. He told her somebody else did the grease-monkey work in his shop, not him, and besides, it was Sunday and he had no intention of working on Sunday.

But Jenny was not one to admit defeat. "If Truman and

Big Boy roll this tire down to your store, will you get somebody in there to fix it?"

Jenny finally talked him down, and the next thing I knew, Truman, Nelle, and I were rolling the tire down the street. Mr. Wiggins had called one of his relatives to meet us at the garage and patch the tube. While we were rolling along, Truman had never lost sight of the objective: Get the tube. He was at times so single-minded and purposeful that it didn't matter what stood in his way: He was going to get what he wanted.

Neither Nelle nor I would have dared think about puncturing Jenny's tire, but now that it was done, we went along with Truman, who had no qualms about the plan. While Nelle or I might have *thought* about doing something destructive, we did more talking than acting. Not Truman. If he had his mind set on something, he rarely let anything get in his way.

Truman said that in order for us to get the tube, we'd need a "diversion." This was the first time Nelle and I had heard that word. We thought it was a French word for stealing. Truman explained, "It means to distract their attention." He said for Nelle to pretend she had a splinter in her foot, and because she was a girl, Mr. Wiggins would pay attention to her. "Hold your foot up to his face and show the splinter," Truman said. This was easy because in the summer, Nelle's and my feet were embedded with splinters and thorns. Nelle sometimes got my mother to pick out her splinters, or her sister, Alice—"Bear" is what we called her.

Just before we arrived at the garage, Truman asked me for my pocketknife. He knew I carried a sharp Barlow. He carried pens and pencils, never a knife. I let Truman have my knife. When Mr. Wiggins got the tube out of the tire,

Truman nodded to Nelle to go into her splinter act. She squalled and squealed and danced around on one foot, holding the other one up to Mr. Wiggins. The garage was dim inside, with only a single light bulb hanging from a cord in the center. It was plausible that Nelle had something in her foot. So Mr. Wiggins dropped the tube and helped Nelle over to the light at the doorway to get a better look.

As soon as Mr. Wiggins's back was turned, Truman whipped out the knife, felt around the tube until he found the nail hole, and made a big slash in the tube. Nelle quieted down when Mr. Wiggins decided her foot wasn't hurt too bad. He came back to inspect the tube and saw this long gash. He knew the tube couldn't be patched, so he called the other Mr. Wiggins to tell him the news and see if he could put a new tube in the tire. Then he had to call Jenny to see if it was all right. He must have gotten a tongue-lashing over it, because we heard him say "Yessum, yessum" at least a dozen times before hanging up.

Mr. Wiggins took out a new tube, inserted it in the tire, and inflated it. When we left the garage to roll the tire back to Jenny's house, the first thing Truman did was gather up the old tube. So that was how we came to have a plentiful supply of rubber-gun ammunition for the remainder of the summer. And Truman came to have revenge on Jenny.

# 8
# The Case of the Mysterious Lady

*I invariably have the illusion that the whole play of a story, its start and middle and finish, occur in my mind simultaneously—that I'm seeing it in one flash. . . . At one time I used to keep little notebooks with outlines for stories. But I found doing this somehow deadened the idea in my imagination. If the notion is good enough, if it truly belongs to you, then you can't forget it . . . it will haunt you till it's written. . . . A little [of my writing] is suggested by real incidents or personages, although everything a writer writes is in some way autobiographical.*

TRUMAN CAPOTE
*in Writers at Work, First Series*

$T$he year I began school, Truman and Nelle were knee-deep reading the Sherlock Holmes detective books. Even though I hadn't learned to read with their speed and comprehension, we three would climb up in Nelle's big tree house and curl up with the books. Truman or Nelle would stop from time to time to read some interesting event out loud. We'd discuss what might happen next in the story and try to guess which character would be the culprit. Sometimes Truman called me "Inspector." Nelle was "Dr. Watson." With his little notebook and pencil in hand, Truman would scribble notes, which he'd hide in his pockets. Sometimes he'd let Nelle read what he'd written, but since I couldn't read, there was no use in showing it to me.

At some point during the day Truman would go back to Jenny's house, pull out the trunk he kept under her bed, take a key from his pocket, unlock the trunk, and hide his papers. He was very secretive about his writing—more careful than virgins with their underwear.

I suppose it was our preoccupation with the detective stories that led us to investigate the mysterious lady. She supposedly was the daughter of Mr. and Mrs. Ralls, who lived across from the Boulars, about a block away from Jenny's house. For some reason the Ralls family and their mysterious adult daughter fascinated Truman at least as much as the Boulars with their reclusive son captivated Nelle and me.

The Ralls family lived in a big, rambling, two-story wooden house filled with boarders. These were people who had left their farms in Purdue Hill, Franklin, Uriah, and the other rural communities around Monroeville and had come to town to find work in the cotton gin, sawmill, school, or mercantile stores. Family members often brought them to town in wagons, dropped them off on Sunday afternoon, and returned to get them on Friday or Saturday.

Mrs. Ralls was a middle-aged woman with boundless energy who cooked three big meals a day for her boarders and for the traveling salesmen who stopped there to eat. She kept fruit and custard pies, pound cakes, and sugar cookies on hand and readily offered these to us when we stopped in for a visit.

Mr. Ralls seemed to be much older than his wife. His hair was gray, and he moved about rather slowly. About the only thing we ever saw him do was feed the calf and mule in the lot behind their house. He bought the calf the day after he sold his big black bull. When we asked him why he sold the bull, he said, "Because he's too old to have calves." We didn't understand this at all, because the bull was gone one day and the calf was there the next day. When we asked him if the new calf belonged to the old bull, he wouldn't discuss it.

Each day after feeding the calf some corn, he caught the mule and hitched him to the wagon. He did this long after the sun was up, a habit we considered disgraceful. We thought people who had farms in the country ought to get up at dawn to do their chores.

In addition to the animal lot in their backyard, the Rallses had one of the finest scuppernong arbors on the entire block. When the fruit ripened to burnished gold in late summer and early fall, we children would go from one neighbor's arbor to the next, pull a handful of juicy, sweet, golden grapes (we called them grapes), suck the juice, spit out the rind and pulp, and compare the neighbors' fruit. Sometimes we'd stop to chat with the neighbors while we were sampling their scuppernongs.

Truman really wasn't a social person who enjoyed visiting or "calling" on neighbors as was the custom in Monroeville and other rural Southern towns in the 1930s. Jenny and Callie did plenty of calling on neighbors, as did Lillie Mae when she was in town. They always wanted Truman to go along and sometimes cajoled him into it, dressing him in fancy linen suits to show him off. Mostly he wanted either to be left alone to play with Nelle and me or to stay with Sook. If he went on excursions around the neighborhood, he wanted to explore on his own and gather facts in the way he wanted.

It was during our daily rounds to the scuppernong arbors that we discovered a robust, wavy-haired young woman sitting with a young man on a bench in back of the arbor. We'd be sampling the grapes and spitting out the pits, when Mrs.

🐛 *Edna Marie Hendrix (third from right) with her family. She married James Arthur Faulk in 1904, when she was twenty-seven and he was eighteen. They became Truman's grandparents.*

🐛 *James Arthur and Edna Marie Faulk with their children. Truman's mother, Lillie Mae, is standing center; Marie is in front of Lillie Mae; Mary Ida is leaning on her father; Lucille is on her mother's lap. Seabon, their only surviving son, is seated on the steps. The year was 1915.*

🐦 *Virginia Hurd Faulk (Jenny) about 1900. A beautiful spinster with a will of iron, Jenny was the bulwark of the family. Jenny and James Arthur's father, Seabon Faulk, Jr., had the same grandfather. Jenny raised Lillie Mae, Mary Ida, and Marie when their parents died. Then she raised Lillie Mae's only child, Truman Capote.*

🐦 Below: *Jenny's home on Monroe Station Road. She grew up here with Sook, Callie, Mary, and Bud.*

*Jenny and Callie at the entrance of their store, V. H. & C. E. Faulk Millinery and Notions. The year was 1912.*

*Jenny and Callie (fifth and sixth from right) bought land and built this new store in 1921, expanding their business to include cloth and ready-made clothes for men, women, and children. The building is on the east side of the courthouse in Monroeville; though no longer in the Faulk family, it is still in use as a business.*

🐦 Opposite, top right: *Born January 29, 1905, Lillie Mae was ten when her father died of tuberculosis. She was fourteen when her mother died of complications after surgery. Lillie Mae was an unhappy, angry young woman when she, Mary Ida, and Marie moved in with Jenny in 1919. Never happy in Jenny's house, Lillie Mae wanted to move out and away from Monroeville. She is shown here at about age eighteen.*

🐦 Opposite, left: *Lillie Mae married Arch Persons at Jenny's house on August 23, 1923. He was almost twenty-five, and she was eighteen. The son of a prominent Alabama family, Arch never lived up to Lillie Mae's expectations. She divorced him after seven stormy years.*

🐦 Opposite, bottom right: *Truman was an adored baby, shown at one year in the arms of Lillie Mae and Lucille.* Above: *with Arch.* Right: *with Seabon Faulk.*

🐦 *Truman with Jenny.*

🐦 Opposite, top left: *Barefoot and still in a sleeping gown, Truman liked to follow Sook to the chicken yard each morning.*

🐦 Opposite, top right: *Mary Ida Faulk Carter, Truman's aunt, didn't believe in children wearing fancy clothes and shoes all the time, as Truman usually did. At her farm, Truman ran around barefoot and ate hunks of watermelon.*

🐦 Opposite, bottom: *Truman in Jenny's flower garden.*

🐦 *The back porch and yard at Jenny's house were favorite places to play. Lucille holds Truman under Sook's watchful eye.*

*Truman atop the rock fence that separated Jenny's yard from that of his playmate, Nelle Harper Lee.*

*By age four, Truman's fears of abandonment were realized. Lillie Mae left him in Monroeville while she sought a new life in New York.*

*Truman in his prized Trimotor Ford airplane, the subject of his short story "One Christmas."*

🐚 *A smiling Truman hugs Queenie, Sook's little terrier. The two are sitting on a bench outside the wash house where he, Nelle Harper Lee, and Jennings Faulk Carter (Big Boy) staged their carnival.*

🐚 *Truman didn't* always *wear Sunday clothes.*

👣 Truman (above) and his cousin Jennings Faulk Carter (Big Boy) (left) spent many happy times together at the Carter farm, where work was done by hand.

*A part-time worker employed by Truman's Uncle Jennings to help with the farming.*

*Uncle Jennings stacks peanuts to dry.*

🐦 *Joe Capote, Lillie Mae Capote, and Mary Ida Carter dine in a New York restaurant.*

🐦 *Arch Persons, who was always scheming and promoting Truman, made post cards of him like this one.*

❧ *Lillie Mae and Joe Capote visited Monroeville at least once a year. They are shown here at the Carter farm on their last visit to see their relatives, in 1952. Lillie Mae died January 4, 1954, shortly before her forty-ninth birthday, from an overdose of alcohol and drugs. Some family members believe her death was accidental. Joe remarried; he died in 1982 at age eighty-two.*

❧ *Truman and his favorite car on another of Arch's promotion cards.*

🐦 *This was one of Truman's happiest days. He came to Montgomery, Alabama, in the fall of 1967 for the filming of "The Thanksgiving Visitor." Uncles, aunts, cousins, and his father, Arch, joined him on the set. A smiling Truman (center) is shown with Mary Ida and her younger son, John Byron Carter.*

🐦 *Home in Truman's later years was the Carter farm in Drewry, Alabama, two miles from Monroeville. He found solitude, family, and a return to his roots in the rural countryside. Spinning tales and enjoying local gossip on the front porch, he spent many hours with his aunt and uncle, Mary Ida and Jennings Carter, pictured here.*

🐦 *Although Truman and his own mother were never close, he found a mother substitute in his aunt, Mary Ida, whom he adored. This photograph was taken at her home while he was writing* In Cold Blood.

🐦 *Truman's deep affection for his Aunt Mary Ida and Uncle Jennings is expressed in this letter, which was written in 1963.*

Darling Mary Ida —

I have been wanting to write you ever since I left you that lovely April morning six weeks ago. I loved being with you and Jennings — you were both so sweet to me, and I was (and am) very grateful for your generosity and kindness.

I have no news, really. The trip was very arduous. But at least I didn't wreck my little car. I saw Arch and his wife in Shreveport. She is very nice. But he really is impossible: I gave him a picture of myself — which he has copied and sent around by the hundreds as an advertisement for his real estate company!!! Now I ask you! I don't really care; but it is embarrassing.

What is my guilt? It's mine and I want it. Because you mean it and because it is beautiful: and I need it — so send it!

Please give my love to all the young folk.

Hugs and kisses, T.

👋 Built in 1928, the red brick Monroe County Courthouse was
the focal point of downtown Monroeville and looks the same as when
Truman Capote was a boy. It currently houses a museum.

👋 Hatter's Mill was built near the turn of the century and was the first sawmill
in Drewry. Daring boys sometimes dove into the pond from the third-story window.
The dam holding back the logs is at the far left end and is not visible in this
photograph. Truman and his friends often swam at Hatter's Mill, the scene of
Edison McMillan's near-tragedy.

👐 *This street scene of Monroeville in 1932 was taken from an upstairs courthouse window. Looking down South Alabama Avenue, eight-year-old Truman could see Jenny's house almost directly behind the post office. The unpainted board house stands taller and bigger than Captain and Mrs. Wash Jones's white-painted house on the left. The roof of Nelle Harper Lee's house is visible just beyond Jenny's house.*

👐 *At the northeast end of the square stood the First Baptist Church, where Truman and Big Boy attended Sunday School. It was the scene of Truman's trick in "Broadway, Act II."*

❦ Jenny's big wooden house burned to the ground in 1937. Many valuable family photographs and personal possessions were lost. Jenny rebuilt this smaller house on the same site a few months later, and Truman often visited here. The house stayed in the Faulk family until it was razed in 1988.

❦ In this letter to Mary Ida, Truman reveals his deep feelings about his Monroeville roots. He hoped to buy a cabin in the woods near Mary Ida to use as a writing retreat. He also maintained a lifelong friendship with Nelle Harper Lee, whose writing talents he greatly admired.

Ralls would come out of the kitchen wiping her hands on a flour-sack towel. She'd say, "Children, this is Mr. Tom Jones, my daughter's husband, who's here from Texas. He'll be with us for a few days."

We'd all smile and shake hands as we'd been taught to do, then Truman would launch into a very adultlike discussion about the weather or what Mr. Jones did for a living. One day after we left the arbor, having been introduced to the fourth or fifth Mr. Tom Jones, and were happily reclining in the tree house with our detective books, Truman said, "Have you noticed there is a different husband every week?"

"Yes, and it's very strange," said Nelle. "Do you think maybe they're not really married?"

"Well, she could marry and divorce and remarry in a hurry," Truman said.

"Naw, not that fast. Not four husbands in a month," Nelle said.

Truman scribbled something down in his notebook. "I have noticed that they do not visit the neighbors," he said. "I wonder why they never call, being newlyweds and all."

When I said something about the daughter not being very pretty, Truman said, "Maybe the woman can't get a husband, so Mrs. Ralls picks out a stranger and introduces him as her daughter's husband just so people will *think* she can get a husband."

"Maybe," said Nelle. "I heard Mrs. Ralls say she wanted her daughter to marry. I think Mrs. Ralls just wants to make us think she's married. The couple probably aren't even friends."

A gleam registered in Truman's eyes. "I know how we can solve this mystery and find out if they're married."

"How?" I asked.

"It's simple," said Truman. "We need to find out if they sleep together."

Listening to his elaborate plan, Nelle and I knew that Truman had already thought this out and had been waiting for the right time to spring it on us. "What we'll do," he began, "is wake them early one morning and see if they both come out of the same room. The daughter lives in that bedroom next to the kitchen, so if they both come out of that room, we'll know they are married. Now if he comes downstairs from the rooms where the boarders stay, we'll know Mrs. Ralls is making all of this up."

"But how'll we wake them to find out?" Nelle asked.

With his hands on his hips and his feet spread apart, Truman said, "You know how touchy Dr. Watson is about his turnip patch. [Dr. and Mrs. Watson lived next door to the Rallses.] You remember how Dr. Watson fussed at Jenny that time when I went into their garden. He told her he'd chastise me if she didn't keep me out. Well, we might as well chastise Dr. Watson with the calf by letting it out. Then we'll knock on the back door and tell Mrs. Ralls that her calf is out in Dr. Watson's turnips. They'll all get excited because they don't want any row with Dr. Watson."

The plan seemed plausible enough, even though I wasn't sure what "chastise" meant. But then Truman was always trying out new words on Nelle and me, and springing new plans on us. He was the leader, and we were the good followers. We decided to get up very early the next morning, which was unusual for Truman because he hated to get up early. So at dawn Nelle, Truman, and I met in Jenny's backyard and slipped quietly down the street. Mockingbirds sang overhead in the big oak trees that grew along the edge of the street. The milk wagon rattled along a block away. One of Sook's roosters crowed. The sweet scent of late-blooming roses from someone's garden hung in the early morning mist. Quiet as church mice, we went to the back lot, opened the pen, and shooed the calf toward Dr. Watson's garden. The calf, hungry for his breakfast, bounded toward the turnip patch and quickly went down row after row of young turnip shoots, nipping them off as he went.

Then Truman marched up the Rallses' back steps and banged on the door. Mrs. Ralls was busily preparing breakfast for the boarders. We could smell coffee and biscuits. She stopped long enough to ask, "Truman, why are you here so early?"

In his most innocent voice, Truman said, "I was up very early this morning, looked out, and saw this calf in Dr. Watson's garden. I thought it might be your calf and I should come tell you."

With a horrified look on her face, Mrs. Ralls flung the pan of fried sowbelly down on the kitchen table and flew to the back door. When she saw the calf she screamed, "Oh, my God! Look at that! Get down here, Ned! Hurry! The calf's out in Dr. Watson's garden!"

The screen door slammed shut behind Mrs. Ralls as she ran down the steps and hurried to Dr. Watson's garden. Next came Mr. Ralls, who bustled around, knocking a chair aside as he tried to hurry out the back door. He hopped and jumped as he tried to tie his shoelaces and run at the same time. Truman, Nelle, and I crept up to the back steps so we could see who came out the door of the daughter's bedroom. But instead of the daughter coming out that door, she came down from upstairs where the boarders lived. She was dressed in a nightgown and housecoat, and her hair was disarranged. She hollered, "Mother! What's the matter?"

At this unexpected turn of events, we hurried back to the garden. The calf was full of turnips, so we didn't have much trouble helping the Rallses run it back to the lot behind their house. All the while Mrs. Ralls was saying, "Thank you, Truman, for telling me. Thank you, children, for helping me get the calf back. Dr. Watson's going to have a fit, but it could have been worse."

With the calf safely impounded, we hurried to Jenny's house and found Sook in the kitchen. She fixed some coffee and cookies for us, and we had a long discussion about the mysterious lady and what she might be doing upstairs where the boarders slept. Sook said, "Now Buddy, Big Boy, and Nelle, maybe it's something we shouldn't talk about. After all, the Rallses are good people and it wouldn't be right to talk about them."

We finished our snacks and headed for the tree house. Truman pulled out his notebook and, in the spirit of Sherlock Holmes, turned to Nelle and me and said, "Inspector, Dr. Watson, now this is what we have. A, Mr. Ralls is too old to have any children. Don't you remember when he sold the bull that he said was too old to have a calf? That bull wasn't near as old as Mr. Ralls. B, this so-called daughter was seen coming down from the upper rooms where the boarders sleep. And C, we also saw her coming out of Barnett and Jackson's Hardware Store last week. So we can reach only one conclusion, wouldn't you agree?"

By this time Nelle's and my eyes must have been as big as Mrs. Ralls's pie plates as we waited to hear what Truman had to say. I hadn't reached any conclusion. I doubt that Nelle had either, but she wouldn't have let Truman know it.

Truman cleared his throat and glanced through the pages in his notebook. Then he said, "She's not the Rallses' daughter at all. She's a traveling hardware saleslady."

Nelle and I must have looked as puzzled as we were, because Truman then defended his position. "You know how difficult it would be for a lady to sell hardware in Monroeville. In order to go on her route and not have people be suspicious, she lives with the Rallses in secret. They need the money she pays for her room and board, so the Rallses pass her off as their daughter. We don't see any damage done in this case so we won't say anything. Is that agreed, Doctor? Inspector?"

We nodded.

Truman put his notebook back in his pocket and grinned triumphantly. "Case closed."

# 9
# Boss

*Talk about mean! Odd Henderson was the meanest human creature in my experience. And I'm speaking of a twelve-year-old boy, not some grown-up who has had the time to ripen a naturally evil disposition. At least, Odd was twelve in 1932 when we were both second-graders attending a small-town school in rural Alabama. All the kids feared him, not just us younger kids, but even boys his own age and older.*

TRUMAN CAPOTE, "The Thanksgiving Visitor"

*I* suppose our lives would have been almost perfect had it not been for a big bruiser of a boy named Boss. He was about the size of Truman, Nelle, and me put together. He had a shock of dark hair, crooked teeth, and a layer of flab over some mighty impressive muscles when he flexed them to show off. Everybody, including we three, tried to stay out of his way. But sometimes that wasn't so easy, because whenever a crowd of kids gathered, Boss and his cronies were in the middle of them. Ordinarily he would have hung around another part of town, but after we convinced Jenny to build us our very own swimming pool, kids were drawn to it like flies to honey. We could hardly enjoy ourselves without Boss and the other kids coming over and hogging it away from us.

There were times when Truman, Nelle, and I would slip off early in the morning just so we wouldn't have to put up with Boss in case he decided to come over for an early swim.

We'd go over to the Rallses' house and pester their mule and eat some of Mrs. Ralls's good food—mostly sweets and cakes. Truman liked cooked greens, fresh peas, and okra more than he did sweets, but at Mrs. Ralls's house he'd eat cakes and drink coffee with Nelle and me. It probably had more to do with the fact that coffee was forbidden by Jenny, and that Mrs. Ralls treated us like special guests. So we'd have something good to eat, then while Mrs. Ralls washed the dishes, we'd go out to their mule lot.

Old Mr. Ralls (our name for him because he looked old as the hills and had cracks in his face) had a barn behind their house where he kept a one-horse wagon. His job every day was to hitch the mule to the wagon and go out to the farm he rented from our cousin, Mary Salter. Since Mr. Ralls didn't stir around until nine o'clock in the morning, this meant that the mule would be in the lot, mean and cranky, waiting on his basket of corn.

Nelle was fascinated by that old brown mule. She liked nothing better than taking a stick and pestering the life out of him by punching him in his sides. She'd crawl on the lot fence and as soon as the mule saw her, he'd lay back his ears, then turn his hind end around, which meant he was about to kick. Nelle would stand at his side and punch him with the stick. He'd whinny a little bit and she'd say, "Look, Truman and Big Boy. I can make him lay back his ears!"

One day Jenny caught us leaning over the fence pestering the mule. She came out of her house on the way to her store and heard the mule whinny. Not one to let something suspicious pass her by, especially when we were nowhere in sight and she heard the commotion from the Rallses' house, Jenny hurried across the street and caught Nelle at her prank. "That old mule is going to kill you children," Jenny yelled.

She grabbed Truman and pulled him off the fence. Then she shook her finger in Nelle's face. "Don't you do that anymore," she said.

We left the Rallses' house and walked to our farm for breakfast. It took us about an hour to get there, considering the time we played along the road, picked dewberries, and talked. We almost talked ourselves into turning around and going back to Nelle's house and opening some cans of Vienna sausage, but we decided that Mother probably had fried sowbelly, grits, eggs, and biscuits. And by that time we were starving.

We didn't pass a soul on the road that morning. Sometimes when we walked to our farm a wagon rumbled by, or somebody galloped along on horseback. Once in a blue moon a car passed us, crunching over the dirt-and-gravel road and kicking up dust. We'd jump down in the ditch to keep from getting run over, then talk about the people. "Wonder who it is? Wonder where they're going? Reckon one day we'll all be riding around in cars?"

There weren't any woods along the road, only open pastures or fields high with cotton and corn. When we turned up the tree-lined road to our house, the sand felt soft to our feet. That's when Truman usually took off his shoes. We loved the way the sand squeaked between our toes and felt cool to the touch.

We arrived at our house about the time Mother had just finished clearing the kitchen, after feeding my father and two field hands, so she wasn't too keen on starting another breakfast. But Truman looked up at her with his big, round, soulful eyes and said, "Please fix us something good, Mary Ida. We're *so* hungry."

"Oh, you poor children, sit down," she said. She took several brown "yard" eggs and cracked them in a blue bowl.

She whirred them around, then poured them in an iron skillet sizzling with butter. My mother cooked on a big wood stove and kept a small fire in it all day, so the leftover biscuits were still warm. We slathered the biscuits with fresh-churned butter and some of the new blackberry jam and ate until we were stuffed. Then Nelle started in on wanting to ride Pal, our horse, a big white-footed bay that was usually quite gentle. I'd ride him or plow behind him for hours at a time.

It was up to me to catch him, and since we didn't have a saddle, we'd have to ride bareback or put a croker sack on his back so his dirty, sweaty back wouldn't stain our clothes. Not that Nelle or I minded, but Truman was the one who wouldn't sit on Pal without something between him and the horse. Nelle and Truman watched while I chased down Pal, put the halter on him, and led him back to the barn. I should have known trouble was on the horizon when I saw Nelle with a stick in her hand, but I wasn't thinking fast enough. For some reason or another, Nelle took the stick and punched Pal in the side. "Lay back your ears," she said, punching him again. But Pal didn't lay back his ears. His nostrils flared in anger. Before any of us knew what was happening, Pal reached over and grabbed the top of Nelle's head with his teeth. He clenched down, and she let out a blood-curdling scream.

Then he reared back, pulling Nelle to her tiptoes. She was screaming and crying, "Help! Help! My scalp's comin' off!" Truman grabbed her overalls, dug his heels into the sand, and pulled as hard as he could, but he was pulling against a furious thousand-pound horse. I grabbed the bridle and hit Pal over the neck. *Whack! Whack!* But the horse kept his grip and pulled.

Screaming in anger and fear, Nelle clenched her fists and

pounded on Pal's neck, but the horse kept pulling back. At any second I expected to see Nelle's head, or at least the top of it, drop to the sand. I whacked Pal with the bridle again and again with all my might, and this time Pal backed away, turning Nelle's head loose. She grabbed her head and moaned in pain. As the saliva from the horse's mouth dripped down her face she must have thought it was her own blood or her brains oozing out.

"My head's bleeding!" she said, with tears streaming down her dirt-stained face. She bent over for Truman and me to look. We pulled aside the short, dark hair to inspect her sticky scalp.

There wasn't any blood. "Nope, you're okay," we said.

By this time the sun was high and hot, and we were hot, dirty, and shaky from our near-tragedy. "Let's go back to Jenny's house and swim," I said.

We all agreed this was a good idea, so we struck out for town. When we got to Jenny's house, none of the neighborhood kids had come to the pool that morning, so Nelle and I jumped in. She immediately put her head beneath the water and rubbed her hair. Truman went inside, but instead of coming out in his swimming trunks, he had kept on his same shorts and shirt and was lugging the small blackboard and chalk Nelle had loaned him the day before. He set up the board beneath the pecan trees. Our splashing commotion and talking soon caught the attention of several neighborhood children, including Boss and his cronies.

"Nelle, you take down their names and get their nickels," Truman said. Truman handed Nelle the small pocket notebook. As the children approached, they handed Nelle their nickels and she wrote down their names in the notebook. Then and only then could they jump into the pool.

By mid-afternoon the pool was full of children. Truman sat on the side of the pool wall, pulled up the blackboard on its stand, and started talking. The fact that he was lecturing wasn't too unusual, because he often did that. He called it "teaching school." Nelle and I liked to play school with Truman, even though we were usually the students and he was the teacher with a lot to say on numerous subjects.

But today was different because Truman wasn't just talking. He had Nelle's blackboard and chalk and was sketching and writing on the board as he talked rather seriously. Because it was late in the summer the children knew they had only a few days left of vacation. They probably wished Truman would just shut up about school and let them get on with their playing, but he was going on and on about it being sinful to kill mockingbirds.

Boss had heard just about enough. He yelled out from the pool, "And why is it a sin to kill a dumb mockingbird?"

In his sincerest, deepest professor's voice Truman said, "Because they eat little colored babies' eyes out."

Boss quit splashing. Quiet settled over the pool. Boss glared at Truman with a dumbstruck look on his face. "So?" he said.

Without cracking so much as a hint of a smile, Truman continued. "With their eyes gone they can't find their mother's nongies. And when they can't see how to nurse their mother's nongies, they'll starve to death. So mockingbirds keep down the colored population."

Boss had a look of murder in his eyes. "I didn't come here to be lectured to, you dumbhead. I came here to swim! Give me back my nickel!"

I suppose we were the last generation that hit first, then talked. If you insulted somebody or hurt their feelings, they didn't start arguing, they started swinging. But Truman was not one to fight, so he turned his back on Boss and continued lecturing and drawing. About that time Boss scrambled out of the pool, grabbed Truman's shirt, and pulled him off his feet. I knew when he grabbed Truman that he would beat him to a pulp, and his cronies would be hard on his heels. I had to act quick. Sure enough, Boss drew back his fist and was about to pop Truman hard in the mouth. That's when I dove for Boss's legs. Then Nelle pounced on him and hit him in the ear with her fist. Boss swooned off balance and fell backward, hitting his head on the cement pool wall. He was out cold on the ground.

Blood spurted everywhere. Nelle and I scrambled up to see how badly he was hurt, and it looked awful. He was limp as a dishrag. But instead of worrying about Boss, Truman was thinking about defending us.

"Go get a butcher knife, quick!" he said to Nelle.

"What for?" she asked, balking at the thought of leaving the scene.

"Just get it. Nobody will convict us if we say Boss was attacking us with a butcher knife. We'll say you wouldn't let him have your favors in the pool, and I was defending you."

Nelle stared at Truman in disbelief. But like good soldiers, we'd do what Truman wanted most of the time, so without talking about it any further, she ran to get the butcher knife. By the time she got back with it, the other children had come out of the pool and gathered around us.

Truman turned to Nelle and said, "Now cut me slightly on the shoulder." Then he thought better of it. "No, you cut Big Boy's hand a little bit. We'll say Big Boy grabbed the knife to keep Boss from cutting me, and then I knocked him out with a hard whack on the chin. And as he fell, he cracked his head on the cement."

Nelle and I started arguing with Truman, especially about the part where Nelle was supposed to cut me with the butcher knife, and all the while Boss lay there in a pool of blood, maybe dead. About that time Boss stirred and groaned. Still dazed, he staggered to his feet. He felt the blood oozing down his face and neck. He clamped his hands over his head and took off running toward home, his cronics close on his heels.

And as he ran, there was a strange look on Truman's face, almost one of disappointment that he didn't get to put the whole scheme into gear.

# 10
# The White Elephant

> *He leaped off the stump, and made for the house, his loosened shirt-tail flying behind; run, run, run, his heart told him, and wham! he'd pitched headlong into a briar patch. . . . the stinging briar scratches seemed to cleanse him of bewilderment and misery, just as the devil, in fanatic cults, is supposedly, through self-imposed pain, driven from the soul.*
>
> TRUMAN CAPOTE, *Other Voices, Other Rooms*

*I* think I'd be giving Truman too much credit if I thought he'd planned this adventure like so many of the others we shared. But Truman was so quick-witted when events and circumstances developed that he could capitalize on them. He would psych us up to see what direction our actions would take. He did this so successfully, even he became infected with the phenomenon.

By this time in our early teenage years, we'd figured out that Nelle was a girl, so she wasn't along on many of our adventures. She was still a great ally at school because she'd hit unerringly with her fist and without flinching. We boys respected this, but we'd begun to do things as a group, and we didn't want Nelle along when we were chasing girls after the Saturday movie or swimming in the creek.

Truman spent a lot of time at our house when his school up North was over for the summer. He was fascinated by farm life—the horses and mules, the planting and gathering of peas and corn, the way we lived without a telephone, electricity, indoor plumbing, or running water. Not that Truman did any work while he was visiting us. While I picked peas or plowed, Truman squirreled up somewhere reading a book. That seemed to be all right with Mother and Daddy. Looking at Truman, you wouldn't think he was a boy who didn't work. He was a tanned, stocky, muscular youth with sun-bleached hair. It was his speech that gave him away. When he spoke, he used perfect English, even as a little boy. He never used slang or local expressions.

Some interesting people lived near us, and they got caught up in our summer adventures. There was Dick Carter, no kin to us, a small, wiry boy who could break a bull calf, harness him, hitch him to a cart, and drive through the woods. He often came to get Truman and me to go swimming at Hatter's Mill.

There was Buddy Ryland, a tall, boisterous, self-centered bruiser of a boy who picked on me unmercifully. When we walked to the school bus together, he was always trying to grab my fingers and bend them back, or looking for something to argue over. Buddy lived with his aunt and uncle a quarter of a mile up the road in a wood-frame house with a cemetery in the backyard. His mother was dead; his daddy was a doctor living in the little community of Eliska. Buddy would visit his dad, steal some of his medicine, and bring it back to "doctor" on Fred Jones and his wife, Bama, the Negro couple who lived in a shack on the Ryland place. One time he "treated" old Fred until his fingernails turned black and fell off.

Fred helped the Rylands and my family in the fields. His wife, Bama, helped my mother with the gardening and cooking. Bama was a tall, slender, light-skinned woman with high cheekbones and a thin nose. She spoke well and could write a beautiful script.

Fred had built a fence of boards and bushes around his house to keep out stray animals and ward off demons and evil spirits. The only opening in the fence was on the south side, and this had a gate that could be closed. About a hundred yards behind Fred's house was a barbed-wire fence separating the Rylands' land from another farmer's. Near this spot was another graveyard, Emmons New Ground Cemetery, with trees so big we couldn't reach around them. In the winter, during let-out time when the cows roamed freely, they grazed over the graves and nibbled the limbs from the trees to about head-high.

Occasionally we boys explored around the cemetery, which stood like a little island in the middle of a great pasture. Big cedars, hickories, and oaks towered above the graves. The trees were so thick at the tops that only the barest bit of sunlight could get through. Depressions in the ground marked each grave site. One time we counted and found about one hundred graves, some dating back to the 1700s. The Rylands always said the west side of the cemetery was for the colored folks, the east side for the whites. There were a few Indians buried in between.

On this particular day, Truman and I'd just finished our favorite Sunday dinner of peas and okra, chicken smothered with rice, and plenty of fresh milk from our cows. Daddy was lying down taking a nap. Mother was in the kitchen cleaning up the dishes, and we'd found a cool spot on the front steps. Dick and Buddy had come over to see us. Buddy, who wasn't picking on me so much anymore, fancied himself to be some kind of amateur doctor, and he was trying to impress us with his medical knowledge. Truman goaded him on.

"*Real* doctors have a skeleton in their office, Buddy. If you are so smart, tell us if you have a skeleton and know the names of all the body parts."

Buddy shuffled his feet and pulled at his pants, which were hanging below his round belly. "Well, n-n-no," he said. "Not a real skeleton. I've got some pictures, though."

We laughed. "Pictures? A picture is not the real thing. Here you are practically living in a cemetery and you don't have a skeleton!"

Now Buddy couldn't stand to be laughed at. He was also one who never let a challenge go unmet. "I *could* have one. I could have one quick if I had some help."

"What kind of help?" Truman asked.

"Digging help," said Buddy. "Let's go dig up one of those skeletons and put it together. Besides, there's no tellin' what else we'll find in there. Maybe diamond rings. They bury people with rings on, ya know. And watches. Maybe's even a pistol lying in there under the dirt."

We looked at each other and knew this was a wonderful idea. Taking some shovels from Dad's tool shed, we struck out walking to Emmons New Ground Cemetery. To get there we crossed a field of new corn working alive with green grasshoppers, and crawled under a barbed-wire fence. The sun was high, shining through tall white clouds. Flies and gnats swarmed in the stifling hot air. A pair of buzzards circled overhead, then lit atop a dead pine tree, watching our every move.

When we reached the cemetery, Buddy stuck his shovel into a depression in the ground, which unmistakably was a grave. "Let's dig here," he said.

"Not there, you idiot!" Truman declared, taking charge. He grabbed Buddy's arm and pulled him back. "Look where you are standing. This is the *east* side of the cemetery. Look up overhead at the sun. See where we are? Over there is the *west* side."

Buddy scowled and leaned on his shovel. "So? What's the difference between the east side and the west side?"

"I thought you said the east side was for the whites and the west side was for the Negroes."

Buddy hesitated and scratched his head. Then he started laughing. "Oh, I get it! Won't be as bad for us if we get caught digging up one of the coloreds."

With that issue settled, we moved to the west end of the cemetery and looked for the right place to dig. "Here," Dick said, stabbing his shovel in the dirt.

"No. We won't get anything but tree roots," said Truman.

I found a place with a small depression. "How about here?" Truman looked it over. "No, that's no good. See how small the grave is? We don't want to dig up any baby." We fanned out and looked some more. We didn't want to dig at a grave clearly marked by a headstone. That didn't seem right, somehow. Graves with trees growing in them were ruled out. We poked around several places before Truman found a depression off to itself. No stone, no tree, or anything stood as an impediment. "Here. This will do fine," he said.

After only a few scratches in the earth, we could see what work this was going to be. The red clay was hard as cement. After two hours, all we had to show for our work was a small dirt pile. We were so hot and thirsty our tongues were parched and hanging out. "Let's go to Fred's house for a drink out of his well," Buddy said. We laid down our shovels and struck out across the field, walking behind the fence, then around to the front entrance. Fred had made a new wind-powered whirligig. This one was a flying duck whose wooden arms flapped when the wind blew. Only today there wasn't any wind. Just deathly stillness. We walked up on the porch and hollered for Fred.

He took his time coming to the door. When he finally opened it, he was pulling up his coveralls, chewing on a piece of broom sage, and talking at the same time. "Whatchall boys want?"

"We're thirsting to death," said Dick. "Mind if we get a dip from your well?"

"Got somethin' better. Bama! Git these boys some Kool-Aid."

We sat on the floor of the front porch, shaded by a tin roof, and waited. There was only one chair, a small rocker made of willow, and Fred sat in that. Bama fixed some grape Kool-Aid and brought it to us in mason jars. We downed it in a matter of seconds. Truman could see that Fred didn't have anything to do this particular Sunday afternoon but chop a little wood for the cook stove. He decided to bring him in on our project.

"Want to help us dig a little hole?"

Fred fanned his shiny bald head with a tattered straw hat. He'd made a hat band from a blue bandanna and stuck a turkey feather in it. "What kinda little hole?"

"A small hole."

"Where dat hole be?"

"In the cemetery up there."

Fred threw up his hands. We might as well have told him the devil was after him. "Lawd have mercy! I wouldn't do that for nothin' in this world. I look up there at night when the moon's out and see all that stuff workin' around in there."

Our eyes got big. "What kind of things are working?" Truman asked.

"Them things. They comes out and goes to workin'. No sah, I wouldn't go in there for nothin'."

Although Fred was convincing, we decided not to give up our mission. We went back to the cemetery, dug and dug, and were about waist-deep in the grave when we realized dark was coming on fast. We weren't about to be in that cemetery at night. Not that we were overly concerned about ghosts, bogeymen, spirits, and demons. But somewhere deep down inside, each of us had a place where terror resided, probably because from our earliest youth we had heard tales from the Negro cooks, some family members, and even strangers eager to tell us what would happen if we weren't good, if we got too far away from the house: Bad man'll git ya!

We got our tools and walked back home, discussing what we'd do with the skeleton when we finally reached it, and where we'd store it. Most important, we swore everybody to secrecy lest the adults find out what we were up to and try to stop us.

It was a week before we could get together and get back to our digging. Dick and I had to help our families with the chopping and plowing during the week. Buddy had to go visit his dad, and Truman had some more books he wanted to read.

The following Saturday afternoon we gathered our shovels and some cardboard boxes to load the skeleton in, and lit out for the grave site. This time we were dressed for the occasion: shorts, no shirts (except for Truman, who always wore some kind of T-shirt and socks), and some tough-soled shoes so we could push the shovels into that hard clay.

We dug and dug. Buddy was the biggest of all and could

do the most digging. After several hours he was in the hole head-deep. We kept expecting to find a coffin, or some kind of debris. By this time, the sun was slanting low, causing shadows to move across the cemetery. It was so dense under the trees, it was almost dark, but not so dark that Buddy missed a gleam of white in the deepest part of the grave.

"Look here," he said, pointing at the white object, then scrambling out as though to escape some terrible evil. With excitement flowing through us, one by one we got down and looked. It was a shell about two inches across with two holes in it.

Truman bent over to examine it. "I think it is a button from a woman's dress. We must have reached her clothes. This means she is under us."

Now we worked even more furiously, fancying ourselves to be archeologists. Using a hoe without a handle, a scraper, and some other small garden tools, we dug out the bones.

"It's the chest cavity," shouted Buddy, pulling out a large curved bone embedded in clay.

"And here's the feet," said Dick.

"Wow!" said Buddy, pulling up the skull and examining the teeth.

"See if there are any gold fillings in them," said Truman. "We need some water to wash these bones. Somebody run up to Fred's house and get a bucket of water."

"You're not leaving me alone in this place," said Dick. So we all went to Fred's house, drew some water from the well, filled the bucket, and came back to the grave. We washed the bones one by one. They sparkled as the red clay washed away. By this time even Truman had forgotten his dignity. He was just as dirty, muddy, and sweaty as the rest of us down in the grave washing bones.

We had failed to note how late in the day it was. The air

was even hotter and more stifling than before. A lone cicada hummed overhead. Some smoke from a distant fire had slipped eerily through the valley and hung over us like a shroud.

All of a sudden Buddy stopped digging. "What's that?"

"What's what?" I said.

"That sound. That rustling." We looked around, but were facing west, so all we could see was the glare of the setting sun. The sun caught the movement of something and flashed its shadow on the tree limbs hanging over us.

"What's that?" Buddy asked again, with more fear in his voice.

"Shhhh. Y'all hush," Dick said. "Listen for a minute."

Truman went on washing bones and tossing them into the cardboard box. He started talking about one of the Tarzan movies with elephants in it. "Did you ever see that movie about how elephants die? When they are old and know it is time to die, they go to the elephant graveyard. For hundreds, maybe thousands, of years they have gone there to lie down and die. With the exception of a few African natives, nobody has ever seen an elephant graveyard."

By this time we were feeling spooky. The shadows were moving. The sun was getting low. The air was cloudy with gray smoke. We were physically and mentally drained from a day of digging and sweating in the heat.

Then, to our horror, Truman suddenly shrieked, "Oh my God! There's a white elephant! He thinks these are his bones and he's coming to get them!"

Terrified, we clawed at the dirt bank, stepping on each other as we scrambled out of the grave. Something lumbered toward us through the shadows. Buddy was the first to scream. "Run! The elephant's after us! He'll get us for sure!"

He took off running to Fred's house with the rest of us on his heels. Ahead was a stand of tall grass and a three-strand barbed-wire fence covered in briars. Behind us were the setting sun scorching our eyes, the deadly beast, and sure death.

Buddy managed to get over the fence unscathed, but as Dick dived under it the barbs grabbed his pants. He pulled and tugged with all his might, shredding the cloth until he got loose. Truman and I dived headlong under the fence. The barbs and briars tore at our flesh and seemed to pull us back to the monster. Yelling at the top of our lungs "The elephant's comin'! Help! Help!" we pulled loose, ran around Fred's fence into the yard, and shut the gate behind us. We were out of breath when we got inside the house. We slammed the wooden door and bolted it. The house was just a one-room shack built up on rocks, with a small side room to cook in, but for now it was our refuge from the monster.

Fred and Bama stood there with terror in their eyes. "The elephant's comin'!" Buddy yelled, hurling his body against the front door as if to hold it shut. Fred grabbed his old single-barrel shotgun that leaned in the corner and crammed a slug in the chamber. Bama screeched and crawled into the bed, pulling the quilt over her. "Oh, help us, Jesus Gawd!" she cried, shaking all over.

A light wind sprang up, making the little whirligigs in Fred's yard turn furiously. The duck's wings flapped; the little man chop, chop, chopped with his ax. Something moved in the shadows. We couldn't see anything but the back of the fence and a few ominous shadows on this no-moon night.

"It's up to the fence!" Buddy screamed, looking out one of the small windows that faced south.

By this time, even though he had to be afraid, too, Truman tried to pacify everybody. "We are here in the house and Fred has a gun. Nothing is going to bother us."

"Ta hell you say!" Buddy popped back. "Listen! And look. See that big eye comin'."

One by one, Dick, Truman, Fred, and I crept around Buddy and dared peek out the window. I was breathing so hard my throat was dry. A large, red eye moved from side to side and seemed to be making its way down the road toward us. "Get that gun up here, Fred," Buddy said in a loud whisper. "Aim it at that thing and shoot or we're all gonna be dead."

Fred took the safety off the gun and leaned the barrel against the windowsill. He put his head against the gun, looked down the barrel, and strained to line up the bead with the red eye moving toward us. "Shoot! Shoot it now!" Buddy said.

The eye came closer, accompanied by the shuffle of footprints on the dirt path. Seconds seemed like an eternity. My heart was pounding so hard I couldn't tell if what I was hearing was my own heartbeats or the thud of an elephant's feet. I expected at any moment to hear the crack of Fred's gun and the furious rage of a wounded animal as it made one last charge—on us!

Then a voice. "Fred. Fred Jones. Are you in there?"

"It's Uncle Will!" Buddy yelled, unbolting the door and fleeing outside. We were right behind him. Will Ryland came into view holding a lantern in his hand.

"What you boys doin' out here so late? Don't you know your folks are worried sick about you?"

Buddy didn't answer right away. He was trying to think of something to say. Finally he stammered, "We—we—uh—was lookin' for Indian artifacts. Yeah, that's what we were doin'."

"Well, come on along with me. Y'all better get home."

We said good-bye to Fred and walked silently with Will back to the Rylands' house. Then Truman, Dick, and I ran all the way back to my house. When we stopped on the front steps to catch our breath, Mother and Daddy heard us and ran outside. "Where've you been? What've you been doing? We've been half out of our minds with worry."

"We were looking for Indian artifacts," said Truman. "We got carried away and stayed out too late."

"Indian stuff!" Mother began, her voice in a near hysterical pitch. "Lord have mercy, Jennings Faulk, all you boys would have to do is walk down the road and kick up some dirt. You'd find all the Indian arrowheads you want without going off in the boondocks and staying out half the night, scaring the daylights out of us."

Mercifully for me, even though Mother and Daddy were upset, they accepted the explanation. Although I knew they wouldn't lay a hand on Truman, I'd get a hiding for sure if they knew the truth. About this time a car came up the dirt road. It was Dick's dad, looking for him. Truman and I glanced at each other, relieved that Dick didn't have to walk home by himself that night.

"Get out of those nasty clothes and get a bath," Mother directed. "I'll put some clean towels in the kitchen. There's some biscuits and ham left from dinner. You boys must be starving."

Even though we were about to drop, Truman and I had to haul in water from the well, fill the bucket, and wash up before we could go to sleep. We gobbled down some biscuits, ham, and cane syrup, then lay exhausted in our beds, afraid to shut our eyes. Because it was summer, the windows stood wide open. Every cricket's chirp, every frog's croak, every scratch of the shrubs against the side of the house reminded us that somewhere out there the beast watched and waited.

A month passed and we boys never spoke of the white elephant. And that was rather unusual, because any other time we'd gotten into some kind of adventure, Truman always debriefed us, asking questions for hours at a time and scribbling in a little pocket notebook. "What went wrong? What could we have done different? If we had done something different, what would the outcome have been?" But not this time.

Toward the end of summer we all got telephones out in the country, and Truman called us from Jenny's one day. "Let's meet on Sunday afternoon, get the skeleton, and assemble it like we had planned to do," he urged. This seemed like a good idea. After all, the original plan was to get the skeleton so Buddy could have it to show he was a doctor.

We met on a Sunday afternoon and made our way through the shoulder-high corn to the grave site. All three strands of the barbed-wire fence were broken where we had crossed it that night. The bones were still there in the box; the tub and our shovels were where we'd left them. Each of us looked into the hole, but we didn't crawl down inside it. We took the bones back to the blacksmith shed at the Rylands' house, spread them on a bench, took some copper wire, and tried to wire the skeleton together. Truman came up with a fold-out photo of a human skeleton with the parts outlined. This made our task somewhat easier. After hours and hours of work, the pile of bones began to look more like a human skeleton.

Truman went back to school in New York a few days later. He packed his trunk, and Jenny took him to Evergreen, Alabama, to catch the train. Our school began too, and

Buddy decided to show off the skeleton. The day he took it to school, students and teachers gathered around and talked in excitement as Buddy displayed the bones in the biology room. Some of the teachers helped with rewiring it, so the skeleton began looking more and more like the real thing.

Everything probably would have been okay if we had kept quiet about where the skeleton came from, but somehow word filtered back to Jenny that Buddy Ryland had dug up one of the skeletons from Emmons New Ground Cemetery. Jenny, who, as a child in 1875 had been to a burial there of some of her relatives, pitched a fit. "You're walking on those graves! Those bones might be some of my kin people!" she shrieked. She called the school principal, teachers, parents, even the probate judge. "It's an absolute sin for you to be displaying that skeleton, looking at the insides of what was once a living person," she said. "And maybe even one of my relatives!"

"Yessum, yessum, Miss Jenny" was all that could be said. The skeleton became an embarrassment to the school, and somebody stuck it in a closet. As far as I know, the skeleton is still there gathering dust.

# 11
# Arch

*The world was a frightening place, yes, he knew: unlasting,*
*what could be forever? or only what it seemed? rock corrodes,*
*rivers freeze, fruit rots; stabbed, blood of black and white*
*bleeds alike; trained parrots tell more truth than most, and*
*who is lonelier: the hawk or the worm? . . . Grass and love*
*are always greener. . . .*

TRUMAN CAPOTE, *Other Voices, Other Rooms*

*T*here wasn't much love in Truman's early life. Being in the
same family with him, I recognized early on that ours wasn't
a family who lavished affection on anybody. It was a family
that worked hard and pinched pennies, but even in hard times
there was always a plate of food and a bed for those who
needed it.

Truman had little love and attention from Lillie Mae, who
had abandoned him. Arch, his father, wanted nothing to do
with either Truman or Lillie Mae. So Truman had to look
for love and family where he found it. Mostly it was Sook
who showed us love. She hugged us, held us in her lap, and
talked to us in our own language of childhood. As we
reached our teenage years, Truman was at our farm on
Drewry Road more and more during his summer vacations.
There he found a substitute mother in my mother, Mary Ida,
and perhaps a little of the father he sought in my father,
Jennings. Mother let him sleep late or curl up with his books.

Daddy didn't make him work or do chores like I was expected to do. Truman wasn't going to sling down bitterweed in the cow pastures, slop through mud to feed the mules, dig fence-post holes, or chop firewood. No, at our house he acted like a guest or favored child, and that's how Mother and Daddy treated him.

When the cook came to our house early in the morning, she and Mother would start picking vegetables in the garden right after breakfast. By nine o'clock they'd have them washed and cooking. We didn't have a lot of meat to eat, but occasionally had fried sowbelly or ham. Mostly we ate crowders and black-eyed peas, sweet corn, squash, okra, tomatoes, green beans, and cornbread. Mother would churn buttermilk, and we'd have sweet milk and buttermilk to drink. Truman loved eating at our house. He'd flatter Mother with "This is *delicious,* Mary Ida."

After Lillie Mae divorced Arch and married Joe Capote, they took Truman to live with them in New York during the school year. Joe was a good and gentle man who tried to get close to Truman. He let Truman have everything he wanted and spent a fortune on him. He bought him the finest clothes, watches, and record players, took him on trips to Europe, and sent him to fine boarding schools. Truman was polite to Joe, but he was never really close to him. For whatever his reasons, he wouldn't let himself like Joe. While I never heard him try to cut Joe down in conversations, he was openly hostile to his own father, Arch.

Truman had a long memory when it came to Arch. When Truman became famous, Arch tried to promote him with postcards that carried a picture of Truman, along with an explanation of him being Arch's son and how close they were. He arranged a big dinner in Mississippi, which Truman agreed to attend. Many people bought tickets to hear Truman lecture. It was a fiasco. A roomful of irate people waited and waited for Truman, who never showed up. Arch finally had to refund their money. And when Arch died, his family held up the funeral for nearly a week thinking Truman would attend. They invited the press to cover Truman Capote coming to his "real" daddy's funeral. Truman didn't go and he didn't send flowers.

Even after Arch and Lillie Mae's divorce, Arch maintained fairly close ties with Mother and Daddy. It probably had more to do with Arch wanting to show off some new automobile he'd acquired because he had "skunked" somebody out of it, or his relentless quest to get some of Daddy's money, which he never did, than with any real affection toward the family. Arch tried and tried to get Daddy to invest in one of his get-rich-quick schemes, or take a trip somewhere with him. Daddy never would say yes or no, and Arch would go back to New Orleans believing he could get something from Daddy.

From time to time Arch showed up unexpectedly at our farm. He'd come roaring up the dirt road, blowing the horn, scaring the cows, and raising Daddy's blood pressure before he ever set foot on the front steps. On this particular day, Daddy happened to be at home at noon, which was unusual, because he was working at a job away from the house. He was rarely home to eat the big meal with Mother and me; the two colored field hands; Bama, our cook; and whoever else might be there.

It just so happened that Truman and Nelle were there that day, too. The colored field hands sat at a separate table in the kitchen while the rest of us pulled up chairs to the long table in the center. Truman could be a wonderful entertainer, and he had launched into telling one of his tales. When he talked he would never hem and haw. His words flowed from one to the other. He'd inflect tones and get so wrapped up in what he was saying, I think even he believed some of it.

He told us he was attending Mammoth Cave Military School, a coed school, and that he, two other boys, and three girls were part of an experiment to see if people could survive for two weeks in Mammoth Cave. Could they stay there the whole time with barest essentials? Would they turn white like a yard plant set in a closet?

He said the students were sealed inside the cave with huge boulders that covered the entrance. Truman told of being scared in the dark, and of their supplies of lights, candles, and rations that had to last two weeks. They had a calendar to mark off the days. Exploring through the cave, they had found colored rocks, lakes, stalactites, and stalagmites. They looked in the small pools of water and caught blind fish. The students raked off their soft scales with their fingernails, then roasted the fish over a small fire built in one end of the cave.

The girls in the experiment had shapely figures draped in scanty clothes. At night, they undressed by lantern light and crawled naked into their sleeping bags. The boys slipped around and tried to catch a glimpse of the girls as they undressed.

When Truman would go too far with his tale, Mother would say, "Shush up, Truman! That's enough, now." Daddy, the colored hands, Nelle, and I would howl with laughter at Truman's descriptions and at Mother's feigned embarrassment. But Truman had great respect for Mother's wishes, and he'd turn the conversation toward something else.

Daddy, on the other hand, liked to bait Truman and see if he could trick him. "How'd y'all go to the bathroom?" Daddy asked.

Eating a helping of the cornbread and beans, Truman didn't waste a second lest he have to admit the tale was all a hoax. "Why, we found a grouping of rocks in one place," he said. "The boys used one side of the rocks and the girls used the other. But there was a terrible problem."

Of course all eyes were glued on Truman, and our ears were tuned in to hear what would come next. Daddy grinned and spoke. "Okay, what kind of problem?" he said.

"Well, down in that dark, clammy cave where it was so quiet you could hear a pin drop, every sound carried throughout the cave. The girls thought we could hear them using the bathroom, and they were too embarrassed. So they just didn't go. The girls nearly died of constipation."

To which Mother blurted out, "Okay, now shush up, Truman. Let's not get too carried away, especially at the table!"

We all laughed until our sides hurt. One of the colored hands laughed so hard he choked. Truman then went on to describe some of the other terrible things that had happened in the cave. The girls grew more and more fearful, so the boys decided to build a huge bonfire to give light and heat inside the cave. They took their packing crates and built a big fire with flames licking the ceiling of the cave.

"But one thing we hadn't anticipated," Truman continued, "was the fact that the heat would cause the stalactites to contract. They would get hot, break off, and pop as loud as a pistol shot. Then they would come flying to the floor like spears and stick up in the cave floor."

About the time Truman was leading up to one of these things falling and spearing one of the boys, we heard a loud car horn in the front yard. The family and Nelle jumped up to go and see about the commotion. It was Arch Persons sitting in a big red Buick convertible. Arch was a wiry fellow with crooked hands and abnormally long fingernails, some of which stuck out three-quarters of an inch. We all crowded around the car welcoming him. He got out, shook Daddy's hand, hugged Mother, and shook my hand; but with the exception of nodding to Truman, he ignored his son. Arch immediately noticed Nelle, who by this time had grown into a tall teenager about as big as he was. Truman and I saw Arch's clawlike hand slip way down Nelle's back as he hugged her. Nelle stiffened, acted surprised, then backed away.

Mother led us back into the house. Arch immediately asked for buttermilk, which he loved with a passion. The field hands had returned to work, and we sat back down at our places while Mother fixed Arch a place at the table. Truman stared across the table at his father. "What's the matter, Arch? Is it the first of the month and your checks are all out and you're going to hide out at Mary Ida's for a while?" Arch smiled and ignored Truman's words.

After he finished eating, Arch offered to take everybody to ride in his new car. "Why don't you take the children?" Daddy said. Mother and Daddy stayed in the kitchen while we followed Arch back outside. Truman and I got into the backseat. Nelle was in the front by Arch, who had pulled her close to him so he could show her how to drive the car. We all rode up the dirt path toward the mailbox. Arch never offered to let either Truman or me drive. He turned the car around, put Nelle under the wheel, and she drove back to the house. Somehow Arch convinced Truman and me to get out of the car, saying he was going to let Nelle drive back to the mailbox. When he and Nelle took off in a cloud of dust, Truman and I stood by the fence and waited.

"What is that man up to?" asked Truman.

"I don't know," I said, "but he's sure acting like some kind of fool."

A few minutes later Arch returned, driving the car by himself and holding a handkerchief over his nose. He got out of the car as Mother and Daddy came out of the house. Arch said he had high blood pressure and that's why his nose was bleeding.

"Where's Nelle?" Mother asked.

"Oh, she wanted to go home, so I let her drive to Monroeville and put her out."

Mother and Daddy had lost track of the time, because there's no possible way Arch could have driven to Monroeville and back in those few minutes. Truman looked worried. I surely was. We ducked out of sight. I knew if Daddy had thought about it, he would have sent me back to the fields to work, so I wanted to stay out of his sight until he left. Then I was going to see about Nelle.

We could hear Arch trying to convince Mother and Daddy to go to New Orleans with him. Mother and Daddy wouldn't have dreamed of going anywhere during the week, but since this was Friday, a weekend trip wasn't out of the question. "I have wonderful connections at the Monteleone Hotel," Arch said. "We'll have a marvelous time, and it won't cost you anything for the room."

"Let's go, Jennings," Mother pleaded. "Arch has been inviting us on trips for years, and we never get to go."

Daddy gave in. While they were packing a small bag, they hollered for me and gave me instructions: Milk the cows, be sure and lock the house, spend the night at Jenny's if you want to, feed the mules, and on and on. All I wanted was for them to leave.

Truman had already thought ahead. He said he wanted to ride as far as Jenny's house with them, so he climbed into the car and spurred them on.

As soon as they left, I ran to the fields and got one of the colored men to milk for me that night. "You can have the milk," I said, "if you'll milk for me until Sunday." He was grateful, because he had a houseful of children to feed. I gave him Saturday off. "Just tell Daddy you worked," I said.

I hurriedly dressed, left the house unlocked so the man could get the jars to strain the milk, and headed to Monroeville on my bike. The two-mile trip seemed to take forever. I was out of breath when I got as far as Nelle's house, pulled in the drive, and ran inside to see about her. Nelle and Truman were sitting at the kitchen table. They were heating Vienna sausages in hot water, spearing them with a fork, and eating them. Nelle didn't look any the worse for wear.

"What happened with Arch?" I asked.

"I drove up to the mailbox and he got fresh. So I hit him in the schnozzle. Then I got out of the car and walked home," she said.

Relieved that Nelle was all right, I joined them in eating Viennas and we talked away the long, hot afternoon, disgusted and puzzled by Arch's actions. By Sunday night I was back at home waiting for Mother and Daddy. They arrived, all right, on Monday morning, and had one of their biggest fusses ever. Little by little they yelled it all out about the trip.

I was so busy worrying about Nelle when they left that I hadn't noticed when Arch put Mother and Daddy's suitcase on the floor of the backseat rather than in the trunk. The three adults had crowded in the front seat. The reason Arch hadn't opened the trunk is that he had filled it with pint bottles of whiskey. He had even put overload springs under the Buick so he could haul more weight. "He must have had a thousand dollars' worth of whiskey in that car!" Daddy said.

"Yes, and we were his cover!" Mother said.

It seems that Arch had a regular bootleg route to New Orleans. He took Mother and Daddy on a junket through little country towns all through western Alabama, Mississippi, and Louisiana. They'd stop at the towns and unload at Arch's bootleggers. They didn't even arrive in New Orleans until Sunday morning. Mother was furious at Arch for taking her off under such circumstances. And Daddy was completely outdone, partly because he feared that the law was going to catch them, partly because he'd been so hoodwinked by Arch.

Arch, on the other hand, had it all figured out. He thought if a lawman had seen him, a lone man sitting in a shining red car in a little country town, he'd invite suspicion for sure. The sheriff would likely come and search his car. But with Mother and Daddy sitting there, and Mother like a tough little bantam rooster so ready to fight or lambaste anybody, Arch felt safe.

Fortunately, they weren't caught. Mother and Daddy were cured once and for all of going off with Arch. And Arch had managed to drive even deeper the wedge separating him from Truman.

# 12
# The Cotton-
# Bale Caper

*My childhood was spent in parts of the country and among*
*people unprovided with any semblance of a cultural attitude.*
*Which was probably not a bad thing, in the long view. It*
*toughened me rather too soon to swim against the current—*
*indeed, in some areas I developed the muscles of a veritable*
*barracuda, especially in the art of dealing with one's enemies,*
*an art no less necessary than knowing how to appreciate one's*
*friends.*

TRUMAN CAPOTE, *Writers at Work, First Series*

*I*n our growing-up years in Monroeville, Truman never
ceased to amaze me with his inventiveness. Although in our
early youth I had learned that he didn't care about other
people's property, I was several years older before I realized
that he was entirely unscrupulous at times. He was a
charmer, and he used that charm to learn the ins and outs of
a situation before capitalizing on it.

Just prior to World War II, cotton was the big crop in
Monroeville. In addition to the big-monied farmers, every
little shirttail farmer in the country had a cotton patch where
he raised a few bales. Horse- and mule-drawn wagons came
into the gin during late summer and early fall. The gin was
just two blocks from Jenny's house and was a great attraction. Lines of cotton-packed wagons waited for their cotton to be sucked up into the gin. People gathered outside
and gossiped while the augers whirred and conveyer belts

whizzed overhead. Cotton dust was in the air as the bales were plunked down for grading. All this was fascinating to country people who didn't see much machinery; it was even a little bit terrifying.

Truman got caught up in the excitement as well, and we spent many hours at the gin watching the goings-on and listening to the talk. People seemed to like gory stories back then as much as they do now. At ginning time, they told about the little girl who had reached over to pluck a piece of lint, but she was too close to the auger, which grabbed her and chewed her arm off at the shoulder. Then there was the colored fellow who fell into the cotton press and was mashed into the cotton bale. They found him dead in the bale a day later when someone spotted a bloody hand sticking out.

Our cousin, Frank Salter, worked at the gin as their bookkeeper. He was Mary's husband. Mary was Jenny Faulk's only married sister. Mary and Frank didn't have any children, and I think Frank was flattered by Truman's attention and interest in his bookkeeping job for the gin. Frank kept up with who owned the cotton in the warehouse, and he went to great pains to explain the procedure to Truman. When the cotton was ginned and baled, each individual bale was assigned a number. A cotton grader sliced the bale, pulled out a piece of cotton, held it to the light, pulled it between his fingers to test the length and strength of the fibers, then assigned it a grade. The weight, producer or farmer's name, and the grade were penciled on a card. Thousands of bales were done this way, making an enormous bookkeeping job for Frank.

The federal government at that time was paying farmers a minimum price per pound for cotton. This was generally above the market price, so it was to the farmer's advantage to take the loan price. Then the government would pay to have these bales stored in the Monroeville warehouse. The government even paid rent on the cotton. Even though the cotton might be sold, it was stored there and wasn't necessarily shipped to the textile buyer.

Frank showed us the locked room where he stored the filing cabinets with small card trays. There was only one door and no windows. Some of the cards dated back to the 1920s. When the cotton was sold, Frank erased the former owner's name and penciled in the new owner's name. Little did I know at the time, but while I stood there innocently taking all this in as passing but interesting information, Truman was hatching one of his biggest schemes.

Truman, who was about fifteen years old at the time, and I had spent several hours at the gin this particular morning. We walked back to Jenny's house for the noon meal. We washed up, took our places at the dining room table by Jenny and Sook, and served our plates with yellow squash, green beans, corn, peas, and cornbread.

"Oh, Buddy, you've got cotton lint all over you," Sook said, fussing over Truman as she leaned over him and kissed the top of his head.

He smiled, obviously pleased at her attention. "We spent the morning at the gin with Frank," Truman said. "He has a very important job managing all the cotton."

"Humph," Jenny growled. "If you can call writing down names and numbers on little cards *work,* I suppose you can say that. Don't know why Mary married him. Oh, well . . ."

When Jenny and Sook finished their dinner and left the table, Truman leaned back in his chair and gazed up at the ceiling. "Know what, Big Boy? It wouldn't be too hard to steal about half that cotton down there."

I couldn't believe what I was hearing. "Hell, man. That's impossible. You and me together couldn't roll one of those bales, much less steal it! You'd have to get an army to tote that cotton even if you could get to it."

A sly grin crossed Truman's face. "You don't have to physically have the cotton to own it. The *cards* are the ownership. All we've got to do is go back in there, and where it says 'Present Owner' write down our names on a bunch of those cards. Then *we* own the cotton."

I thought for a moment. "But don't you know that whoever owns that cotton has a copy showing that *he* bought the cotton? We couldn't claim it."

"That's true," Truman said, taking a bite from a honey-colored tea cake. "But if you think about it, that cotton has changed hands many times. There's probably a hundred people who owned this cotton at one time or another. So if *we* changed to the present owner, anybody who owned the cotton would have to check every piece of paper to see if our number was the one they actually owned."

"That's possible," I said. "But it wouldn't do us any good to claim ownership because nobody would pay us boys rent on the cotton. The rent money would still go to the warehouse."

We talked long into the afternoon while we walked downtown around the square and stopped for a soda at the drugstore. Then we sat for a while on the benches near the courthouse. The unfocused plan buzzed about in our heads. Then Truman had a revelation about how he'd involve his stepfather, Joe Capote, who owned Putnam Textiles, a company that supplied thread and yarn to a textile company in the Carolinas. "I've got it," Truman began. "Joe likes to speculate. We'll have these bales put in the name of Putnam Textiles. Instead of having the bales stored in the warehouse, we'll have these sent to the textile plant. We'll arrange a sale in the Carolinas and send a notice to Monroeville saying to get our cotton from the warehouse and ship it to the Carolina mill. Then the mill will pay Putnam Textiles and we'll have money for the cotton. By the time the real owners check the numbers and decide *they* really own it, why, it'll be too late. We'll select cotton that's real old, and chances are they'll never know the cotton is gone."

The whole project seemed too involved and over my head. "Well, how much cotton do you think we could sell?"

"At least a thousand bales."

"A thousand bales! Why there probably isn't much more than that in the warehouse."

"Yes, you're probably right. A thousand would attract too much attention. Let's do it with a hundred."

"Well, that's more like it," I said, still unsure.

"All right. Now this is the plan. We'll break into the storage room and get into the files. We'll find some of the oldest cotton and put the name of Putnam Textiles as present owner. When I get back to New York next week, I'll take some of Joe's business stationery and write to the textile companies to see if I can sell the cotton to them cheap. Then I'll type up the orders, send them down to the warehouse, and have them ship it up to the buyer. When the money comes into Joe's company, I'll claim it somehow."

The thought of money sent a tingle all through me. I'd rarely had any money. As a child of the Depression years born and raised in the country, a little change or a couple of dollars was the most money I'd ever seen at one time. Truman was talking hundreds, maybe thousands, of dollars. Then I remembered the portable record player and records Truman had brought to Jenny's house that summer and the hours we'd spent listening to "Old Man Mose Kicked the Bucket." Truman must have been reading my mind.

"When our money comes in, I'll buy you the finest record player money will buy and send you a stack of records," he promised.

"Yeah. So what do we do next?"

"First thing is I've got to learn to write like Frank. If there's any strange handwriting on the cards, Frank will be suspicious."

That night while Jenny was down the street visiting with neighbors and Sook was in her room, Truman nosed around Jenny's desk and found a note written by Frank. He studied it judiciously and practiced for hours until he learned to write a flowing script just like Frank's. We waited until Saturday, the busiest day of the week at the gin, to find Frank.

"Now when I convince Frank to unlock the door, you walk with him over to the card file and keep him distracted for as long as you can," Truman said.

I agreed. When we spotted Frank, Truman made up some story about how he was going to build a file and needed to take a look at the way the little card trays fit into Frank's file. Being accommodating, Frank took the file-room key, which, during business hours, hung loose on a large wooden sign outside the office. He opened the door. I ran ahead to the card file and asked a question to distract Frank's attention from Truman. Frank had left the key in the big brass lock, so Truman slipped it back out and quickly pressed it into a bar of soap. Truman winked at me as a signal that he was ready to leave. We said good-bye to Frank, then ran ahead out the door while he locked the door behind him.

As we walked back to Jenny's house, Truman took the soap out of his pocket. The key's depression was clear and he was obviously pleased. "You know that pan where Jenny keeps all the old keys? Let's get it down and see if we can find one like this. If we find a near match, you can file it down and we'll have a key to unlock that door."

After supper that night, Jenny and Sook retired to the living room to listen to a radio program. Truman and I went to the room where I had a small wooden work table to build model airplanes. Truman mixed some plaster of Paris and poured it into the soap mold. While the plaster of Paris hardened, we scratched around in the old pan filled with all shapes and sizes of keys.

"Here's one!" Truman said, excitedly pulling out a large black door key.

Then he pried the molded key loose from its soap bed. The two keys were the same length and circumference. We would have only to file a small notch in the door key. I brought out a file and smoothed a place in the key. The filings fell away as the key took proper shape. "I believe that's it," I said, holding the key beside the plaster of Paris mold.

"Let's go in tonight," Truman urged. "It's Saturday, and there won't be much action. Besides, school will start soon, and I've got to leave for New York before next weekend."

Truman took Jenny's flashlight from the kitchen drawer and with the newly made key in hand, we slipped out the back door into the black night. We walked along the sidewalk listening to the crickets and glancing from side to side to see if anyone was watching. There were no policemen in

Monroeville in those days. Occasionally the sheriff came by on his way to some bootlegger's house to see if he could catch someone in the act, but no watchful eyes were looking that night. The last movie was over at nine o'clock. After fifteen minutes, when people had time to walk home or go to their cars, the town became quiet as a tomb.

"What about the night watchman at the warehouse?" I asked, feeling nervous.

"We'll hide out and see when he makes his rounds," Truman said reassuringly.

We left the safety of the neighborhood behind and walked briskly toward the cotton gin. A large hanging light illuminated the entrance to the gin where the cotton wagons rolled up. But the warehouse area was black as soot. Truman and I crouched in some bushes and waited. The night watchman came along and walked toward the warehouses. His heels clicked on the gravel, and we held our breath when he stopped close by. Then he turned and walked away.

"He's gone," said Truman. "It'll be five or ten minutes before he's back here, so let's go."

We hurried to the dark, locked room. I held the light while Truman slipped the key in the lock and gave the door a nudge. Nothing happened. He turned the key again. This time the door opened and we slipped into the warm, musty room. We carefully shut the door behind us. "Shhhh. Don't let the light shine under the door," Truman said. I handed Truman the light. "I'll go stand near the door and listen," I said. No sooner were we in place than the night watchman approached. I hissed, and Truman snapped off the flashlight. The watchman walked slowly by. My heart pounded as I heard his footsteps fade into the distance.

Truman took out a little notebook with pieces of carbon

paper inside. Using flowing script handwriting like Frank's, Truman wrote "Putnam Textiles" on the cards, then the number of the bale. He had a record of each transaction. After what seemed an eternity, he shut the last card file.

"Let's go," I said, anxious to get away before we were discovered.

"Not yet," Truman whispered. "The watchman is due back any second."

Soon the watchman's footsteps came closer. He paused before the door, placed his hand on the knob, but didn't turn it. Then his steps trailed off one last time. Truman and I gave him time to get out of sight, then locked the door behind us and strolled back to Jenny's house. Just before we entered the house, Truman whipped the little notebook out of his pocket, tore out the carbons, and handed them to me. "If something happens to me, then you're the owner of one hundred bales of cotton stored in the warehouses in Monroeville, Alabama."

Truman left for New York the next week, and I went back to the farm. Two weeks passed before I was back at Jenny's house spending the weekend. It was about seven o'clock on a cool Saturday night in mid-September. I was dressed and ready to walk out of the house to go to a movie when the phone rang. Jenny answered it. "It's for you, Big Boy. Some girl's calling 'Jennings Faulk.' "

"Hello," I said.

"Don't let on like it's me," Truman said, desperation in his voice. "I had the operator ask for Jennings Faulk so Jenny wouldn't know it was me calling."

"Okay," I said, "so what's up?"

"I . . . I . . . oh, everything's gone wrong!" Truman sobbed. "Joe found out about our scheme. We were about to pull it off. Our letter even convinced a Carolina firm to buy the cotton. But then they called Joe about it, and when he dug into everything, you know what he found," Truman said, choking on the tears as he tried to get out the words.

I had heard Truman cry only once before, and that was a long time ago, when we were little boys. "Well, what happened?"

"Joe and I had this awful screaming fight. I thought Joe was going to hit me, but Mother started yelling and stepped in. You've got to help me, Big Boy. I'm begging you. Joe says if I don't get those cards changed back, he's going to cut off my allowance and put me in public school. Pleeease, Big Boy. Please say you'll do it. Tell me you'll go out there tonight and change the cards back like they were before. If anybody finds out about this, I'm ruined for good."

Luckily I'd kept the door key. It was on my work bench along with the carbons and bale numbers. But to go back alone, in the dark . . .

"Listen to me, Big Boy," Truman began, trying to talk between sobs. "Do just like we did before. Take the flashlight. Look out for the watchman. Take a towel or old cloth with you and stuff it up under the door so if you're working on the cards and don't hear him as he makes his rounds, he won't see the light under the door. When I changed the cards, I shielded the light with my body. But you'll need something under the door. Please tell me you'll go."

"You're asking an awful lot, Truman," I said, whispering so Jenny, who was in the other room listening to her radio program, wouldn't hear. "It's too risky. I could get caught, and then what?"

"Stop and think what will happen if you *don't* do it. If I'm exposed, then you'll be exposed. It's that simple. You've got to do it. If we get found out, Mary Ida and Jennings won't ever let you come back to town on Saturday night."

The thought of not being able to get off the farm and come to town to spend the weekend at Jenny's house, go to the movies, and pal around with friends was more than I could stomach. "I'll try. That's all I can say." Then I hung up the phone. I picked up the key and carbons from the bench, took the flashlight, and went to the movies to kill time. I hung around the theater until the last movie was over so I could know when the streets would be deserted. Then I walked to the gin and hid in the bushes just like before. This time as I watched and waited, the watchman came by with two buddies and a bottle of whiskey. They sat on the front steps of the gin office and drank and cussed until late into the night. My head nodded with sleep. I knew if I stayed there another minute I would lie down in the bushes, sleep until morning, and perhaps be discovered. So I waited until I thought the men weren't looking my way, slipped out of the bushes, and went back to Jenny's house.

The next morning I awoke early. The streets were deserted except for a few people delivering milk. I dressed, took the key and carbons, and walked boldly up to the locked room. The sun was just coming up as I glanced around for the watchman and his buddies. But they were gone. Unlocking the door, I slipped in and locked the door behind me. Silently but quickly I went through the files, pulled the cards, and matched the numbers. I didn't attempt to erase the Putnam Textiles name at the bottom, but scratched through it with the pencil as though it were a clerical error that had been corrected. I worked and worked until my back hurt from hunching over. Finally everything was put back into place.

I waited and listened near the door for a few seconds. A blue jay cawed, a car passed by, and a cow mooed in the distance. I didn't hear voices or footsteps. Then I turned the key, stepped outside, and locked the door behind me. I felt the weight of the world lifted from my shoulders as I walked back to Jenny's house. The sun warmed my back as I whistled "Dixie." Then I tossed the key into some weeds on the side of the road.

*I*n later years, after Truman became wealthy, Joe Capote was arrested for embezzling funds from the corporation for which he was the bookkeeper and treasurer. He was bonded, and the bonding company paid the corporation, but then the bonding company sued Joe for this money, about $100,000. Truman had a pang of conscience about the possibility of Joe going to prison, so he came to Monroeville to talk with Mother, Daddy, and me about Joe's predicament. He asked, "Do you think I should pay Joe's bond money to keep him from going to jail?"

Daddy, who was always rather stingy anyway, asked Truman, "How long would Joe be in prison?"

"Maybe eighteen months," Truman said. "But he may get out after serving only a few months."

"Well, Joe couldn't hardly make that much money working during that length of time, could he?"

Truman agreed and did not pay the money. I think he had in his mind all along to let Joe go to jail, but wanted to cleanse his conscience. Joe served almost a year. For all of Joe's upset about Truman's stealing the cotton, he didn't seem to have any qualms about embezzling from his own company.

As for our cotton-bale caper, the massive buying, storing,

and selling of the cotton was done by the Monroeville Bonding Company in offices at the bank, and from a master list. Frank Salter's card file was only the first identification of the bale and was not used as a permanent record of sale.

Once again the laughing fates were looking over our shoulders.

# 13
# Lil George

*Without warning, a strange thing happened: the man reached out and gently stroked Kay's cheek. Despite the breathtaking delicacy of this movement, it was such a bold gesture Kay was at first too startled to know what to make of it: her thoughts shot in three or four fantastic directions. . . . After a little, he lowered his hand solemnly and sank back in the seat, an asinine grin transfiguring his face, as if he had performed a clever stunt for which he wished applause.*

TRUMAN CAPOTE, *A Tree of Night*

*T*his particular day in the middle of summer, Dick Carter and his helper, Charlie McCants, were tired of plowing. Dick thought if he could get up with some of us boys we could go swimming or maybe scratch up a nickel to buy one of Sally McMillan's candy bars. Sally bought cartons of shredded-coconut candy bars from Mr. Pugh's "rolling" store [goods sold from a cart]. Then she'd sell them to the children or field hands and make a little profit.

The bars must have been pure pressed sugar candy, because it was so sweet it would hurt your teeth. You had to take your time and chew it real slow. A bar would last a long time, so we thought it well worth a nickel. The bars were wrapped in different colors—red, green, white, and blue—but they all tasted the same.

Sally was strict about her business: no credit to anybody. Sally said her husband, Big George, made plenty of money and that her candy business was "jest a sideline." The people

Big George worked for picked him up on the main road every morning at daylight and didn't bring him back until after dark, so he wasn't around during the day. It was just Sally and her two-year-old roly-poly baby, Lil George, alone all day in their shack in the woods. Sometimes Lil George wore a flour-sack diaper tied around his chubby behind; other times he crawled naked in the dirt.

Edison McMillan and I were picking peas in the garden when I heard Dick and Charlie galloping up the road in a cloud of dust. I knew if I stayed around much longer I'd get rooked into shelling the peas, too, so I was glad to see them. Truman must have been ready for some action as well, because he put down one of his favorite books and walked outside to see what we were doing. Dick said, "I'm gonna get Buddy [Ryland]. Y'all catch up Mary and let's go to ride."

"Okay," I yelled back. I put down the basket of peas and motioned for Edison and Truman to follow me to the barn. The only way I could leave was to slip off from Mother, so I tried to be quiet. Down in the barn I caught Mary and held her while Truman laid a gunny sack over her back. "Is it true you can get ringworm and all kinds of diseases from rubbing against mule skin?" he asked.

I said I didn't know.

"Even if you can't, then when she starts sweating, I can't grab on with my legs unless the sack's there."

His argument was reasonable. Sounded just like Truman. Making up excuses but not ever telling the whole truth. I figured it had far more to do with Truman not wanting mule hair sticking to the insides of his legs than with any excuse he gave.

I crawled on Mary's back, extended my hand to Truman,

and helped him up. He squirmed around, looking a little out of place in his silky T-shirt, socks, and sandals. You could see the little tracks in his short blond hair where he'd combed it.

Edison caught Ida, the other mule, and we rode off in the direction of Hatter's Mill. We made it as far as the main road, when we caught up with Dick and Buddy on one mule and Charlie on another. Truman fished around in his pocket and pulled out some change. It wasn't just a nickel or dime but several dollars in change. I saw the money and thought it was ridiculous for him to have it. If we other boys had had any money, we would have left it at home for fear of losing it.

Truman stuck the change back in his pocket, then said, "Charlie, I wonder if Sally still sells that coconut candy."

"She sho does. Like to have me a taste of it, too."

We all agreed we'd like to have some candy, because that was one treat we rarely had. Only nobody but Truman had any money.

"I'll give a quarter," Truman said.

There were six of us, so even though each one wouldn't have a bar of candy, there would be enough to share. As we rode along, we discussed Sally, the candy lady. She was black as midnight, with a fluff of shiny, curly hair swirled on top of her head. She was tall, full-figured, with breasts the size of watermelons now that she was nursing Lil George. We had seen women nursing before, but nobody we'd ever laid eyes on had breasts the size of Sally's.

Living out in the country, we knew some things early on about nature. Like the merciless way the old rooster chased down the hens and stomped them half to death at mating time. We'd helped bring over the neighbor's bull to service the cows. And we'd watched calves, pigs, and goats being born. All of us had milked cows before. It was nothing to grab the firm teat, guide the warm milk into the bucket, and feel it dribble down our wrists and palms. And there in the cow stall to smell the odors of manure, urine, hay, kerosene, and milk all mixed together.

Still, the sight of Sally's huge breasts intrigued us teenage boys, who were beginning to feel the sap rising. As the mules clopped down the sandy road, we questioned the workings of nature. "Wonder what her milk looks like? Tastes like? How much milk does she give?"

"Look at the size of her tit compared to a cow's bag," offered Buddy. "Sally's got to give a gallon a day. Got to. Any good cow'll give a half gallon at a milkin'."

"But she don't give it all at one time," Charlie said. "Lil George nurses all the time, so she lets it out a little bit at the time."

Dick laughed. "Looks to me like Lil George is gittin' mighty big to still be nursin'."

Truman replied, "Well, you know why she still nurses, don't you? She can't get pregnant and have another baby so long as she is giving milk."

"Is that a fact? You reckon Big George don't want no more babies?" Edison said.

Buddy, who professed to be worldly, said, "Naw, it's Mr. Pugh, the rolling store man. Sally eats up most of that candy, and she can't pay him when he comes by to collect. So he just takes out in trade what she owes for the candy."

That remark took a little digesting. Then Dick said, "You don't reckon Mr. Pugh gets the milk when he gets the trade, do you?"

"That white trash? Him and Sally?" said Charlie.

We laughed so hard we nearly fell off the mules, because Mr. Pugh was a scrawny man, unshaven, with long, straggling hair and discolored teeth stained from chewing tobacco. He'd try to spit through the few teeth he had, so tobacco juice always dribbled down the corners of his mouth. He wore dirty, ragged coveralls and old beat-up boots. Our mental picture of Sally and him together was about more than any of us could stomach.

About once a week Mr. Pugh clanged and banged down the road in his horse-drawn store loaded with pots and pans, jugs of kerosene, cooking oil, and barrels of sugar and flour. He'd stop in front of a house, and if anyone asked for something he didn't have, he'd grunt and say, "Ain't got it." Sometimes he'd take trade in those hard times, though. A frying chicken or tough old laying hen were all the same to him. He'd take a chicken for a quart of kerosene to burn in the lamps. But you had to bring your own jar. One time we boys had a string of fresh fish we'd caught at Hatter's Mill pond, and we tried to trade him our fish for some candy. "Nope, don't want 'em," he said.

Later we learned from Sally that he'd trusted her with a whole box of coconut bars, which lent credence to our suspicions about the two of them.

When we rode near a grove of cedars, Charlie reached up, grabbed a branch, and plucked off a hard, green, round berry. "See this here. If Sally don't want no more babies then all she has to do in the middle of the month, halfway through the full moon and no moon, is eat one of these cedar berries."

We laughed and poked fun at Charlie. "If she ate one of those cedar berries she'd be so sick she wouldn't let nobody have any," Buddy said. "Besides, a woman can't have a baby but in the middle of the month anyway. Halfway between the new moon and no moon, if she won't do anything then, she won't have a baby."

We turned the mules into Sally's clean-swept dirt path and saw her sitting in a rocker on the front porch of the two-room wooden shack. A separate weathered outhouse stood about fifty feet away, and we caught a whiff of the vile odors. The yard was shaded by a big oak tree heavy with green acorns. At first glance we could see that she was nursing Lil George on a breast so big the veins bulged out. She wore an old muslin dress open at the front. Sally made no pretense about the feeding, even though we stood there goggle-eyed at the scene. She merely grinned when we got off the mules and stopped short at her front steps.

"What y'all want?" she asked, fanning herself with a dog-eared paper church fan.

Buddy cleared his throat. "We want to buy some candy, but we ain't got but a quarter."

Sally pointed at each boy and counted. "One, two, three, fo, fi, sik. Which'un is gonna do without?"

Truman shuffled his shoes about in the sand and stuck his hands in his pockets. He brought out a shiny quarter and held it out to her. It was bargaining time. "Couldn't you give us each a bar and take off your profit?"

Sally thought for a moment. "Well, for you boys, I reckon I can. Tell you what, I could get a bar myself and we can all share in the profit."

We liked that idea and waited to see what would happen next. She pulled the breast away from Lil George, left him on the chair, and went inside to get the candy. When she came back she hadn't covered herself and made the situation worse by bending over to show us the different-colored bars in the box. We tried to look at the bars, and not stare at her, but her flopping breasts kept getting in the way. After looking from bar to breast to bar and back again a dozen times, we selected the candy we wanted, unwrapped the cellophane, and started chewing. Sally flopped back down in the chair, and Lil George went back to sucking. She bit off a huge hunk of a red bar and, like everybody else, greedily started chewing. We were about dizzy and could hardly eat for all the rocking, chewing, sucking, and fanning.

For some reason Sally pulled the nipple out of Lil George's mouth. He decided he didn't like this abrupt interruption, so he reared back and let out a big squall. She nonchalantly reached into her mouth, got a wad of the candy she'd been chewing, and before Lil George could get out another yell, she plopped the gooey, partially chewed candy into his chubby mouth. At first he looked pleased and started smacking his little round cheeks. But as soon as he drew a breath he gagged and choked. He tried to throw up the candy, but it stuck in his throat. We stood there in shock.

Sally jumped up and started screaming, "Help! Somebody help!" She grabbed Lil George and shook him. He turned red in the face and his eyes bugged out, but he still couldn't catch his breath. By this time it was dawning on us that the situation was serious. We jumped up on the porch but nobody seemed to know what to do. Sally shook Lil George again and screeched, "Help! Lawd, help!" but nothing happened to make Lil George breathe.

Then Truman yanked a handkerchief out of his pocket (which was unbelievable because none of us carried a handkerchief except in the dead of winter when we had a cold, and then we called it a snot rag). Truman's handkerchief was a Sunday-go-to-meeting one with a nice hem. He wrapped the handkerchief around his right index finger quick as a flash, stuck his finger in the baby's mouth, and fished around until he got the candy out.

Finally, after what seemed like an eternity, Lil George caught his breath. Without ever pausing, Truman turned to Sally. He lifted one big breast, stuck the wad of candy beneath it, then wiped her breast all the way down from her shoulder to the nipple, as though milking it. She was petrified. She even quit chewing, and some of the candy oozed out of one side of her mouth.

Truman looked Sally in the eye. "Lil George won't choke now."

"Yessuh," she said. "You's right. He won't choke now."

Then Truman turned around, calm and straight-faced. I half expected him to bow, but without saying a word he got on the mule. The rest of us followed suit and fled down the road.

Even though Truman had pulled off a slick one, he wasn't as cool about the whole thing as he pretended. As we rounded the bend and headed out of sight, I looked back to see the gunny sack lying in the dirt by Sally's steps. He hadn't thought about that sack in his hasty retreat, but had straddled the bare back of that grimy old mule like the rest of us.

# 14
# Hatter's Mill

*I settled with relatives, a cotton-growing family who lived in a remote part of Alabama: cotton fields, cattle pastures, pinewoods, dirt roads, creeks and slow little rivers, jaybirds, owls, buzzards circling in empty skies, distant train whistles—and, five miles away, a small country town. . . . I was walking in a forest along the bank of a mysterious, deep, very clear creek, a route that eventually led to a place called Hatter's Mill. The mill, which straddled the creek, had been abandoned long ago; it was a place where farmers had brought their corn to be ground into cornmeal. As a child, I'd often gone there with cousins to fish and swim. . . .*

TRUMAN CAPOTE, Prologue,
*Other Voices, Other Rooms*

One scorching hot summer day Dick Carter yelled outside my kitchen window, "Hey, Big Boy! Let's go swimming at Hatter's Mill." He and his colored helper, Charlie McCants, were each straddling a mule lathered from a hard gallop down Drewry Road. They had been plowing when, nearly overcome by the heat, they unhitched the mules and raced to my house two miles away. My mother looked up from the bowl of black-eyed peas she had been shelling, wiped her hands on her faded, blue-flowered apron, and opened the screen door.

"Big Boy's in here helping me," she called. I put aside the green beans I'd been snapping and stood beside Mother at the screen door. In the distance we saw Edison McMillan coming up the path with yet another basket of beans from the garden.

Sweat was dripping from Dick and Charlie as they sat bareback on the mules. "C'mon. Let's go swimming at Hatter's Mill," Dick said.

I looked at Mother, hoping she would agree, but doubting she would let me out of the job at hand. "We've got all these peas and beans to put up," she said in dismay. "I'll be over that hot canner half the night as it is. Oh, all right, go on. See if Truman wants to go along. He needs to get out and get busy at something."

I was so happy to be rescued from the kitchen I hardly knew what to do. "Give me a few minutes," I said to Dick. "Truman's in the living room reading. I'll have to get him. Then catch up the mule."

"Okay," said Dick. "I'll go see if Buddy Ryland wants to go. You wait here, Charlie."

Dick rode off in a cloud of dust. Edison had reached the house by that time and was left staring at a basket brimming over with beans. "I sho nuff would like to go along with them boys," he said to Mother. She smiled at him. "Okay, Edison. But first do your train imitation for me."

Edison grinned. "Why, Miz Carter, I didn't know you knowed about my train."

"The boys said you sounded just like the mail train passing through Drewry. I want to see you do it."

Edison was a gangly black boy with sinewy arms and legs and wide-palmed hands. He had a smiling face planted on a small head, about the size of a grapefruit, leading some of the older folks to say "He's a boy whose body has outgrown his mind." He was mildly retarded, but he worked and played along with the rest of us boys.

He was especially good at imitations, and enjoyed the praise for doing them. Edison started huffing and puffing. He flailed his arms like the connecting rods going to train wheels, and he shuffled his feet on the gravel path. "All aboard!" he said, then blew a loud whistle between big, white teeth. He went forward before applying the brakes and squealing the wheels to a halt. Slowly he reversed, *huff puff, huff puff, huff puff*—then faster as he trotted backward. He puckered his lips. "*Whoo whoo. Whoo whoo. Whoooo whoooo.*"

About the time he finished the choo-chooing routine, Truman walked in and we all applauded. "Great!" said Truman. "I didn't know you were so talented."

"It ain't nuthin'. I jest practiced a lot," Edison said. He crawled up on the mule beside Charlie. "See y'all over to the Rylands' house."

As the two rode off, I started out the back door to catch Mary, the mule. "Do me a favor," Truman called. "Grab a gunny sack for me to sit on."

Down in the mule lot I enticed Mary to come over by holding out an ear of freshly shucked corn. She was a good mule, at least compared to Ida, the stubborn one nobody wanted to plow behind. Sometimes Ida would squat down in the middle of a row and refuse to budge no matter how many obscenities we yelled at her ("You cussed, stubborn, damned ole mule!"), or how much torture was threatened ("I'll strip your hide off! I'll crack your skull wide open! I'll break your legs if you don't get up and plow!").

I found a clean gunny sack to drape over her back, grabbed her mane, and crawled on her. I went back to the house, held out my hand, and pulled Truman on behind me. Mother waved good-bye from the kitchen as she called, "You boys don't stay too long. And be careful down at that old mill pond, you hear? Stay away from the deep part and those snaky pilings. You might get hurt—or worse. Promise me."

"See you for supper," Truman said. "We'll be clean as new pop whistles."

Down on the main road Truman and I caught up with Dick and Buddy, Charlie and Edison on their mules. It was a hot deep summer day as we meandered slowly down the narrow sandy road. On either side of the ditches, tall honeysuckle and Virginia creeper vines covered briars as high as the mules. Beyond this tangled growth stood a forest of young pines and some cotton fields. We had gone about as far as the mailbox when Charlie spied something in the road and yelled, "Stop! Don't go another step!"

"What's the fuss?" I asked, slowing Mary's gait.

"Look! There 'cross the road! See that track," Charlie said, excitement mounting in his voice.

We stopped, slid off the mules, and walked over to see the long, wide impression that stretched all the way across the road. It looked as though a saucer had been dragged on its edge through the soft sand.

"Gah-o-o-ly," said Buddy. "It's a monster snake track. That's what it looks like. What kind you reckon it is?"

"Maybe a king snake. They're harmless," I said.

"Or it could be a big ole moccasin heading toward the mill pond," Buddy offered.

"Ain't no moccasin that big and wide," said Charlie, who seemed to know an awful lot about snakes.

"Looks like a big rattlesnake to me," said Dick. "Ain't no other snakes got that wide a belly and could be heavy enough to spread the sand apart like that."

"Then don't nobody move," said Charlie. "That's probly

what it is—a big granddaddy rattler. It's a bad omen. No, it's worse than that. It's a terrible omen."

"What we gonna do?" asked Dick.

"Ain't but one thing to do. Gonna X it." Cautiously Charlie approached the track.

Truman, who had been sizing up the situation, offered, "Why don't we just go around it?"

"Oh, no! Ain't no way 'round it. Not in them tall briars. 'Sides, that ole rattler's probly layin' in there right now a-lookin' at us and sizin' us up. He's got his ole poison tongue lickin' from side to side, ready to jab us. Kill us!"

"So let's just go back," I said.

"Naw, I tole you I'd X it." Charlie stuck his big toe out and drew a large X mark across the snake track. Then he bit the end of his tongue to draw saliva and spat in the X mark. "All right now, y'all do the same. Y'all spit in the X."

One by one we tried to work up enough spit on this scorching day to place our mark on the X. Charlie was satisfied. "Now we can cross it. The evil's gone."

We crawled back up on the mules, started out again, and were soon out on the main road. We walked down the hill, past Mr. Hatter's house and store, and soon arrived at the mill with its thirty-acre dammed-up mill pond. Both the dam and the mill had been built of pine timbers near the turn of the century, but now, in the late 1930s, Mr. Hatter only operated the mill on certain days. Today was not one of them. Sometimes people took a picnic lunch to the mill, spread a blanket on the ground, and spent a peaceful hour. But today nobody was in sight, not even Mr. Hatter.

We tied the mules to a shaded hitching post so they could nibble weeds. Then we entered the bottom floor of the mill and stepped over the brown sacks bulging with meal. These were the tolls Mr. Hatter exacted from each farmer. He kept one-eighth of each farmer's corn in exchange for grinding.

This was the first time we'd visited the mill when it wasn't grumbling with the grinding operation. Ordinarily, the grinding rocks were on, with one huge rock turning through a series of big pulleys and belts. The only way to be heard over all the noise was to shout.

The wood-board dam, supported by a series of A-frames set four feet apart, stretched from the corner of the mill house across the creek. It looked very much like a twelve-foot-high wood fence with a narrow, four-inch-wide top. There was a sheer drop down into the footings. Water could run over the top in bad weather, so around the slimy footings were hollowed-out places that were treacherous and deep. Beneath the dam the water was dark and snaky.

In the past, we'd seen some of the older, more daring youths jump from footing to footing, or jump from the window on the bottom floor of the mill to the water ten feet below. This was the area where the water came out of the pond and into the raceway down to the turbine, so it was deep and cold.

We explored a stairway leading to an upper section of the mill. A big open window in this area was at least fifteen feet above the mill pond. Truman pulled off his silky blue T-shirt and sandals, rolled them together, and handed them to me. Then he crawled into the window. He swung his arms back and forth in front of his muscular chest and took several deep breaths. "Watch me," he said. "Did you know I am an expert diver?"

When I realized he was about to jump, I was terrified. It was too far for a young boy to dive. But before I could yell "Stop! It's too dangerous!" Truman had touched his toes, sailed through the air, and sliced the water like an arrow. He was under for several seconds, then emerged laughing and hollering. "Wow! Feels wonderful! Come on in!"

Infatuated with the feat, Dick, Buddy, and Charlie hung over the window trying to decide if they should risk it, too. It seemed safe enough. Edison, meanwhile, slipped like a squirrel down the shaft and ran around the mill. He stood at the edge of the dam and said, "Man, I believes I could steam down that dam." He huffed and puffed up a head of steam.

From his place in the water, Truman called, "Don't try it, Edison. It's too slick and narrow."

"You're nuts if you think you can do that," Buddy called below.

But Edison steamed and puffed. His drive rods were going. His wheels were spinning. Blowing, whistling, and flailing his arms, he came from under the mill house to the top of the dam. His wheels spun about twice before *sploosh!* He was over the edge in a flash, into the footings and pilings.

We were horrified. We ran as hard as we could down the shaft, out of the front of the mill, across the road, all the way up to where the creek got shallow, then up to where Edison had fallen in. He was nowhere to be seen. Truman, who was still in the water and had a better view of where he went in, said, "Dive for him! There!"

We dove and dove, risking snakes and timbers around the murky pilings. Every time we came up empty-handed. "Godalmighty! Where is he?" yelled Buddy in desperation. "How could he just disappear like that?" Charlie wailed: "He's dead. He's gone. Edison's gone. Oh, what we's gonna do?"

"Hush up!" Truman said. "You go tell Mr. Hatter a boy is hurt in his mill." With that, Charlie took off running to

Mr. Hatter's house, and Truman took a deep breath and dived for Edison.

Precious minutes passed and still no Edison. "He's gone," cried Dick, fighting back tears.

"Keep diving," Buddy said, spitting water. "We can't lose him like this." Again and again we went under. I was weakening. My arms were numb from swimming. My chest ached from holding my breath underwater. My legs were so tired they could barely kick my body back to the surface. I knew I had gone as far as I could go. But Buddy wouldn't give up. One more time he disappeared beneath the surface. This time he didn't come back so soon.

I could hear Dick crying out, "Come back, Buddy, not you, too. Come on, Buddy."

Then a head emerged. A mouth pointed to the sky, spit water, and yelled, "Help! I got him! I got Edison!" Buddy had grabbed hold of Edison's suspenders and was trying to get his head out of the water.

"He's dead," Buddy cried. "He's dead."

Truman took charge of the situation. "Get him over here," he yelled. "Now listen. Sometimes a person who has drowned looks dead on the outside but has life on the inside. They are like a hot coal that needs air to bring back a flame. We need to get the water out of Edison, get some air in him, and maybe he'll start to breathe."

"But how? What do we do?" I said.

Truman said to lay Edison across the footing. "Big Boy, you get on his arms and pull up when I tell you. Buddy, you get on his feet and push down when I say. I'll count and tell you to push. Are you ready?"

With what little strength we had left, we began to push and pull. Truman counted, "One thousand one, now pull.

One thousand one, push. One thousand one, pull. One thousand one, push." We pulled and pushed and pulled and pushed. Water gushed out of Edison's mouth. "Keep going," Truman said. "One thousand one, push. One thousand one, pull. One thousand one, push. One thousand one, pull." Minutes dragged by as we worked on Edison. We were so tired we were about to pass out from lifting Edison's arms and legs, which were as heavy as water-soaked logs.

Edison didn't budge. Finally Truman said, "I hate to say it, but we might as well quit. We tried as hard as we could to save him."

We backed away slowly, looking at Edison lying limp as a rag on the footing. Tears welled in my eyes. My throat tightened as reality set in. Truman, Dick, Buddy, and I made our way back to where the water was shallow, crawled up on the bank, and lay back. Each of us groaned with his own personal agony.

Then, a cough. Another cough. The sound was too far away to be from one of those lying on the bank. "Who's making that noise?" Truman asked. We looked toward the water. Edison was up on one elbow, coughing and trying to breathe. We looked at one another in disbelief. "It's Edison!" we said, swimming to him.

Truman, the strongest swimmer, reached him first and slapped him on the back. "Help me get him up," he said to us. We gathered around and helped Edison sit up. Edison coughed and took some deep breaths. "How do you feel?" asked Truman.

Edison nodded. "Okay." He was weak, but not so far gone that he couldn't pucker his lips, lean back his head, and wail, *"Whoo whoo. Whoo whooooo."*

# 15
# Broadway

*There's just this I want to say, Buddy. Two wrongs never made a right. . . . What you did was much worse: you planned to humiliate him. It was deliberate. Now listen to me, Buddy: there is only one unpardonable sin—deliberate cruelty. All else can be forgiven. That, never.*

TRUMAN CAPOTE, "The Thanksgiving Visitor"

*W*hen Truman came to Jenny Faulk's house in the summer of 1943, he was full of tales about pornography movies he'd seen when he'd gone with Lillie Mae and Joe to visit Joe's people in Cuba earlier that year. After living with the Capotes in New York City and going out on the town with them on numerous occasions, Truman could describe the red-light district in Manhattan to the nth degree. He told Buddy Ryland and me about the scantily clad ladies of the night who openly walked the streets as prostitutes. All this talk was fascinating to us country boys who had never seen more than the edge of a girl's slip showing beneath her dress. Or maybe a bra strap that had fallen off her shoulder. The only place we saw low-cut dresses, sensuous lips, and alluring buttocks was on the movie screen. We would gladly have died an early death to have seen some of the sights Truman described.

At nineteen, Truman had a fine-toned body, tanned muscles, and chin hair that he shaved off every now and then. I used to wonder why he didn't date. He was handsome enough for girls to want to be with, but to my knowledge, he never dated anybody in Monroeville. I used to wonder if he was afraid to ask a girl out for fear she'd turn him down. He had another fear, too—a fear of physical pain. A bloody nose, black eye, or some cracked knuckles were painful, and Truman wasn't about to experience any of those uncomfortable things. When he was young, he got Nelle or me to do his fighting for him. As he got older, if he saw a fight brewing, he'd run away.

We boys didn't hold the fact that Truman was a coward against him, probably because he made up for it in other ways, like telling us about the exotic sights he'd seen in Cuba and New York. He'd spoon-feed us tales, and we'd lap them up. Truman had an intense drive and curiosity about girls and sex. It was a great quest for us to see how far we could go with a girl and what you could see, which wasn't much, because the girls we knew had mothers who guarded them. Some of us might get close enough to hold hands with a girl during the movie, or sneak a peek down her low-cut dress, but that was about as far as it went.

In the early 1940s, in an isolated place like Monroeville, Alabama, nobody came into contact with any movie stars. We lived for the movies on Saturday night, where we saw the heroes and heroines and their glamorous life-styles. A lot of the girls in our town yearned for such a life, dreaming of careers in Hollywood or on the Broadway stage. If we gathered at the drugstore, the topic of conversation usually centered on how a girl could leave the farm life behind and find fame and fortune as an actress.

Now Truman was a person who would capitalize on anything he thought would help him have his own way. This time he wanted his way with a certain attractive female named Missy, who sometimes sat with us in the drugstore. She had long, flowing brown hair, slender legs, a full bosom, and a movie-star smile. She also had an overly protective older brother, Ham, whom Truman saw as his way to get to Missy. One day Truman and I were in the drugstore with Ham drinking a cherry Coke. Truman was talking a blue streak about what he could do for sixteen-year-old Missy, if only Ham would persuade her to cooperate.

"Big Boy tells me you just graduated from high school, Ham," Truman began. "That's great. Got any plans, like signing up for the army?"

Ham took a long swig of the cherry Coke and twirled the straw around in the glass. "Yep to the first question, nope to the second," he said. "I'm going to the university and study medicine. My folks don't want me to join up. I don't want to either. Don't want to do any fightin'. If I'm studyin' medicine, the army won't come lookin' for me, figurin' I'll do 'em more good in the long run if I know how to sew up the bloody bullet wounds."

All this talk of bullet holes in human flesh turned Truman's face pale. He fidgeted, then quickly changed the subject. "I've been meaning to talk to you about something. You know I've been living in New York with my mother and stepfather, Joe, don't you?" Ham nodded. "Here," Truman said, opening a sack of peanuts and shaking some of the salty nuts into Ham's broad hand. "Well, one of Mother and Joe's very good friends, Mr. Marshall, is producing plays on Broadway. Marvelous plays. I've seen every one of them. But you know what? There's not a girl in any of them as pretty as Missy. No sir. Not a girl in any of them as pretty as your very own sister."

Ham swelled with pride. He smiled and took another drink of the Coke, then munched on the peanuts. "You don't say. Did you tell this to Missy? She's always talkin' about how one day she'll make it big in show business." Truman shook his head as Ham continued. "I knew she was pretty, one of the all-time school beauties, but I never thought about her being as pretty as the girls on the Broadway stage."

"She is, you just trust me on that," Truman said. "I've a discerning eye about beauty, especially now that Mr. Marshall has commissioned me to scout for talent while I'm traveling around the country. He's interested in seeing fresh new faces and exciting new talent. He'll make overnight stars out of the girls I recommend to him."

Ham's eyes were as big as saucers. He poked a prideful chest out beneath his blue-striped cotton shirt. "It's too bad," Ham said. "I guess her beauty'll be wasted on us country boys."

"Now hold on a minute," Truman said, seeing an opening. "I just might be able to help Missy."

As Ham slurped the last of the Coke, he managed to get out the word "How?"

"First of all, I'd be interested in knowing if Missy has any talent," Truman said, clearing his throat. "You know, if I'm going to recommend someone to Mr. Marshall, I'd have to see for myself what the talent was."

"Missy ain't got no talent," Ham said.

I nudged Truman's leg beneath the pine table. I didn't want to blurt out into the conversation, but I thought Truman should know something about Missy that I knew.

Truman looked at me. "Do you know of any talent Missy has? Is she musical, or limber as a dancer?"

"Kind of," I said. "That night we had the barn dance, I saw her dancing with some of the older boys, and she surely looked pretty and graceful. So I know she can dance."

"Wonderful!" exclaimed Truman. "That's just what we're

after! Beauty and gracefulness. Now how could we see her perform?"

Truman looked at Ham, whose dark brown eyes stared back stupefied. Ham wasn't about to volunteer his sister for any scheme.

"Think about it as a way for your sister to achieve what no other girl in Monroeville could ever achieve, Ham—a place on the Broadway stage. Think of it. Her name emblazoned in lights across the marquee. Everyone would be dressed up and standing in line to buy tickets to see Miss Missy perform. Just think of it!"

"I-I-I don't know," Ham began.

"Oh, come on, Ham," I urged. "Give her a chance. What's there to hurt?"

Ham thought another minute or so. "Well, okay, but if you want to see her, you've got to abide by my rules. Is that clear?"

Truman grinned. "Oh, perfectly. Why, we wouldn't think of doing anything illegal, would we, Big Boy?"

I shook my head.

"These are the rules," Ham began. "First, you can't get too close. You'll have to observe from a distance. And it can't go on too long."

"Okay. I can agree to that. So where could we do it?" asked Truman.

"The best place would be the horse barn behind our house," said Ham. "There're two stalls back there and a little tack room. Truman, you and Big Boy can get on the far side of the horse lot, and that'll put you about a hundred feet from the tack room. Missy can come out of the tack room and perform a little dance there. C'mon to my house. I'll talk to Missy and see if she'll agree to do it."

Truman winked at me. We left the drugstore and walked

along in the warm summer day, kicked pebbles aside in the dusty road, and talked about the dancers Truman had seen in Cuba. They were dark-skinned, bare-breasted women with fruits piled high atop their heads and scantily clad men beating sensual sounds on skin drums. When we reached the barn, Ham told us to stay on the far side of the lot. He went inside the house and in a few minutes emerged with a smiling Missy at his side. She squinted at the bright sun and waved at Truman and me across the horse lot.

She seemed nervous as she looked around the smelly barn, picked up a handful of fresh straw, and piled it atop a mound of horse droppings. Inside the tack room, she pushed aside a heavy western saddle, some blankets, boxes, and boots to make more room for herself. Then she propped open the tack room door. Imagining music playing in the background, she gracefully twirled around several times in her fluffy yellow skirt, shuffled her sandaled feet in a jaunty little dance step, waved her arms upward, and blew a kiss. Truman, Ham, and I applauded, whistled, and called, "More! More! Encore!" When she curtsied, her long, glossy hair fell almost to the floor. Then she laughed and ran back into the house.

Truman was ecstatic. "See, Ham! See what a wonderful actress your sister is? She's a born performer."

"Yeah," I said. "She'll look good on Broadway." Ham grinned. I think he believed us.

A week later I was sitting in the drugstore, sipping a soda I'd charged to Jenny and talking with Missy. While the overhead fan chased away flies and the muggy July heat, I gazed, mesmerized, into Missy's bright green eyes. I didn't even see Truman come in and lean over my shoulder. "Missy, Missy, Missy!" Truman began. "You were absolutely marvelous! "Your performance was one of the grandest I've ever seen. In fact, I've been on the phone talking to Mr. Marshall in New York and telling him all about you."

Missy glowed. Her cheeks flushed, her eyes danced with anticipation. "What did he say?"

"He's interested, all right. There's just one teensy little problem, though," Truman said, demonstrating by holding out his thumb and forefinger. "I need to see a little more serious skit. If you get the part in Mr. Marshall's play, you'll be pretending to be a striptease dancer. So what I need is to preview how you'll react in this situation. It's nothing personal, of course. This is all theatrics. In your own mind, just say, 'This is an art form and there's nobody out there watching me.' "

Missy was startled. "You mean you want me to *take off my clothes?*" she said slowly, blushing and nearly choking on her Coca-Cola.

Truman didn't answer directly, but took a napkin and drew what he wanted her to do. He sketched the inside of the barn and said, "We'll do just like we did before. We won't get close enough to see anything that may embarrass you. Big Boy and I'll be across the lot like before. But we'll have to do this so Ham won't know."

She still hadn't agreed as Truman continued with the plan. "We'll put a record player in the tack room and it'll have a blues record on it. When you start the record, you'll look out and see us across the lot. Then you do a striptease like you think it ought to be done. Don't undress like you were going to hurry and jump into bed, but drag it out and entice the audience as you take off your clothes. When you've removed all your clothes, turn around and bow to the audience in the opposite direction. Think you can do that for me? I just know I'll have a good recommendation for Mr. Marshall when you finish."

Missy slowly nodded her approval. "Ham is supposed to help Mr. Feagin in the garden tomorrow, so he won't be around all day," she said.

"Good. That's good," said Truman. "Big Boy and I'll be at your house at noon. The record player will already be in the tack room. When you get in there, turn on the record player and look out the door for my white T-shirt. When you see me wave it, then you start the music and your routine."

"If you like what I do, then you'll say some good things to Mr. Marshall about me?"

"I sure will," Truman said. "He's depending on me to find some new talent for him, and I think you're the right person."

"Okay," she said, her smile full of hope. Then she finished her drink and left us.

As soon as she got out of sight, I grabbed Truman's sleeve. "Sit down here. Have you lost your mind?"

Truman laughed and took a seat beside me on the metal chair. "Piece of cake," he said. "You'll get to see some sights tomorrow that nobody in Monroeville has ever seen. Not even the girl's own mother!"

"But it's so deceitful! Truman, you're really a scoundrel, you know it? Missy is a good girl. An innocent girl. To deliberately trick her like this, well . . ."

"Oh, pshaw, Big Boy. Don't be such a ninny about this. You'll get an eyeful just like I will, and don't say you won't enjoy it."

"Well, I'd be lying to you if I said I didn't want to see her in the raw. It just seems wrong to be tricking her. You don't have any connections with a Mr. Marshall at all, do you? You're just making all of this up."

"Haven't you ever heard about all being fair in love and war?"

I mumbled that I'd heard it somewhere.

"Are you with me on this or not?" insisted Truman.

"You know I'm with you. I've been with you through thick and thin on everything else."

Truman slapped me on the back. "That you have, cousin."

The next day, Truman and I arrived at Missy's barn a few minutes before noon. I was curious about the large brown bag he was carrying, so I asked him about it. He opened the top of the sack and I peeked in. "What's that thing?" I asked.

"You'll see," Truman said, pulling off his white T-shirt and handing it to me. "As soon as Missy comes out on the porch, you wave this white shirt and let her know we're here." Then he ran around to the back of the barn. He got behind a crack between the stall and tack room. Although I didn't know it until later, he opened the sack and removed a small movie camera. About this time Missy opened the tack room door and looked in my direction. I waved the white shirt. Then she started the music.

As the blues music whined a tune, Missy unbuttoned her blouse one button at a time, exposing her bra. She unbuttoned her skirt and let it fall to her feet, then stepped gracefully out of it. Slowly she unbuckled her sandals and stepped out of them. Then she slid her blouse off her shoulders, took off her bra, pulled down her slip, and then stepped out of her pale blue panties.

As the music crooned on, Missy gyrated, moved, and bumped around and around in full view. She looked like what I thought a hootchy-kootchy dancer would.

As Missy was preparing for the grand finale, which was

to turn her backside up to the audience, I spied Ham stalking out the front door of the house. He must have seen our truck parked at the house and put two and two together. He slammed the door behind him and was walking so fast he was almost running toward the tack room. A tall, lanky guy who could be mean as a hornet, Ham was out for blood. I jumped out of the shadows and frantically waved at Truman.

Missy just happened to look up before she stuck her seat out the door. When she caught a glimpse of her brother angrily striding toward the barn, she fled back inside the tack room and bolted the door.

As I started running across the horse lot to warn Truman, I hoped Missy was yanking on her clothes. But I arrived too late. Ham already had Truman by the neck and was choking him. "I'll kill you, you little sneak! How dare you take pictures of her! By damn you're not talking any pictures back to New York and have people laugh at my sister!"

I grabbed Ham's arm. "Wait! Wait! It's nothing, Ham. We weren't doing anything," I yelled, still unaware of the movie camera.

With that, Ham turned on me and was about to hit me when Truman fled, dropping his expensive camera. Ham grabbed the camera and threw it after Truman as hard as he could. "You forgot your damned camera!" he yelled as the camera smashed against a post. The dark film spun out in the straw. Then I realized what Truman had been up to.

By this time Truman was out of sight, Ham was grinning victoriously, and Missy had emerged, fully clothed. She was breathing so hard she could barely speak. "Now Ham," Missy began, "we weren't doing anything but a little skit like we did the day before. There's nothing wrong with what we were doing." Then she saw the smashed camera and started crying. "You probably ruined my chances to go to Broadway, Ham. How could you do this to me?"

Ham put his arm around Missy's shoulder. "I didn't mean to ruin things for you, Missy. I just got so mad when I couldn't find you. Then I thought I saw you in the barn. I was afraid the boys were up to no good. I didn't want you caught up in anything bad."

*"Nothing happened,"* she insisted. "And besides that, it's all over. Truman'll probably never speak to me again."

"Good!" said Ham.

While they were discussing things, I picked up the smashed camera and quietly slipped out of the barn. I would have taken the film, too, only Ham was standing on it and I figured I'd better leave well enough alone. But I didn't need a picture to remind me of all I'd seen that day. The nude picture of the prettiest girl in Monroe County burned in my brain.

# 16
# Broadway, Act II

*The host releases his hawk, sends it soaring. Vincent thinks, no matter, it is a blind thing, and the wicked are safe among the blind. But the hawk wheels above him, swoops down, claws foremost; at last he knows there is to be no freedom.*

TRUMAN CAPOTE, "The Headless Hawk"

*I*t took Truman a year to get back at Ham. I don't know what excuse, if any, Truman gave his stepfather about the smashed movie camera. Truman didn't mention it, and I wasn't about to. I do know, however, that in Truman's mind, Ham had insulted him and he would find a way to repay in kind, no matter how long it took. Truman never forgot any little slight he thought had been done to him, and he surely proved it by his actions toward Ham.

That summer of 1944 when Truman came to Monroeville was the last time he and I had our little adventures together. In later years when he came to see us, he was a successful adult and an altogether different person. This particular summer was also the last time he saw his beloved Sook, for she died a little over a year later.

Truman's parents had sent Truman abroad again, probably thinking they could keep him away from the draft. During the time he was gone, Lillie Mae, who was an alcoholic, got drunk and burned the chest where Truman stored his writings and papers. All the little notebooks, stories, and writings that Truman had kept since childhood went up in one furious flame. Truman was selfish about his writings. He rarely showed anybody a line of it. If he did let anybody read it, he would then fold it and lock it away in this little chest. I never knew why Lillie Mae got so furious at Truman. But they had never gotten along, and this was her final way of getting back at him, for whatever reasons.

So when Truman returned to New York after his visit to Europe, it was to a disturbed alcoholic mother, and his writing chest in a pile of ashes. I cannot imagine that this was a happy homecoming. But the worst still lay ahead of him. Joe lent Truman his car to come and visit us in Monroeville. Truman arrived on a weekend, and I happened to be staying with Jenny and Sook. Jenny had gone for the afternoon, and only Sook and I were there when I heard him drive up. He parked the big black car in the driveway and looked around. The old house, the one he'd spent so much time in, had burned several years ago. Jenny had built a new house on the same foundation, but the new house just didn't have the same *feel* of home that the old house had given us.

Truman got out of the car, smoothed his hair, tucked his shirt down in his tan trousers, and bounded up the front steps. He wanted to look his best after a long, hot drive. I met him at the door. We shook hands at first, then hugged.

He slapped me on the back with, "Hey, Big Boy! When are you going to stop growing up and start growing out?" We laughed. I was a bean pole, and even though he was short, he was muscular and filled out.

Hearing voices, Sook came down the narrow hall. At seventy-three she had begun to get feeble. Her eyesight was going. She didn't seem to be as alert and full of life as she once was. When she saw Truman she didn't smile or open her arms as she had done so many times before. He ran to her just the same. "Sook! Oh, Sook! I've missed you so much!" he said, grabbing her with all his might and nuzzling his head against her chest.

Sook didn't respond. She just stood there for a few moments. Then she held him at arm's length and looked at him. "My, my, Truman, you're grown. You're grown now." I could see in her eyes that she was through with Truman. He saw it, too, and it must have cut at his heart like a dagger. Her "Buddy" was no longer the magic young person, and never would be again. He'd crossed the threshold into manhood and was one of those strange adults that Sook didn't know how to respond to.

She gave him one last look as if to say good-bye, then turned and walked slowly back to her room muttering, "Grown now. You're grown now." She disappeared down the darkened hallway. Truman never spoke to her or saw her again.

Tears welled in his eyes and spilled down his face as he looked long after her. I knew he wanted to run to her, have her sweep him up in her arms and kiss away all the hurt. *I* wanted to run to her and find comfort, too. But that was to be no more. Neither of us knew what to say. This was so totally unexpected for him. Although I had realized during the past year that Sook was drawing away from me, it was a gradual thing, not a sudden, shocking thing like this. Finally, after what seemed an eternity of standing there, I said, "Let's go out to Mother's house and eat supper. Spend the night with us. Mother and Daddy will be so glad to see you."

Truman seemed relieved. He blew his nose and we got into the car and headed out on Drewry Road to the farm.

We didn't talk about Sook and our hurt feelings. It seemed to be a subject too sensitive to dare approach. I wish we had talked it out. Not that Sook could help herself; I knew she couldn't and I think Truman was intuitive enough to know it, too. But talking might have helped us both understand our feelings and diffuse some of the anger I knew Truman had to be feeling.

When we approached the house, Truman started honking the horn, scaring Daddy's cows so bad I doubt they gave any milk that night. Mother came out to see about all the commotion, and when she saw Truman, she went into hugging and kissing him. She asked what he had been doing. He got a few words in, then she quickly moved off the subject of Truman and on to Lillie Mae and Joe and how they were doing. Several of Truman's short stories had been published, and he wanted some praise for his accomplishments. He particularly needed some comfort and solace after his rejection by Sook. But Mother wasn't going to dote on him. She asked him how long he intended to stay.

"Only a couple of days," he said.

Then she said, "Well, I'm glad you came this weekend. Ham's getting married in a huge wedding at the Baptist Church. I know you'll want to go to the wedding and reception with us."

Truman grinned.

Mother put Truman in the front bedroom. That was his favorite room. It had a view of the daylilies, the green pastures, and the little road that went up to the Rylands' house. We had a good supper that night of fresh peas, corn, okra, tomatoes, and hot cornbread. After supper, Mother, Daddy, Truman, and I sat outside on the porch a long time talking. Truman told us little stories and anecdotes that kept us laughing for hours. He used several voices when he did this.

One voice was his own Truman voice, which he used in everyday conversation with us. He also had two other voices. One was a high-pitched, female-sounding voice, which he used when he wanted to play the part of a woman in telling some little story. The other voice was gritty, gravelly, and full of bass. He could boom out loudly. It was a voice that would make the hair crawl on your back.

After entertaining us Truman told us he was glad to be back home. He told us all about Lillie Mae burning up the little chest, and how disturbed he felt about her behavior and her drinking. Mother wasn't sympathetic, which didn't bring Truman any comfort. Mother had always nurtured some resentment about Lillie Mae, but now wasn't the time to be taking the I-told-everybody-so attitude. We all agreed that we didn't know what could be done about Lillie Mae's abuse of alcohol, and now drugs. Truman just felt sad about it.

We went to bed early. I was so tired I fell right to sleep on the cot beside his bed. Not Truman. Being a night owl, he read for hours by a single electric light bulb. One time I heard him snickering, so I rolled over and asked him what he was laughing at, figuring he'd found something humorous in one of the books he was reading. All he said was, "You'll see tomorrow, Big Boy." Then he turned off the light.

For breakfast the next morning Mother fried bacon, cooked grits, made biscuits, and scrambled fresh brown eggs. Truman kissed Mother on the cheek. She kissed him back. "We missed you all last year, Truman."

"Didn't you get my cards and letters?"

"Sure did. Saved every one of them, too. I'm just glad you're back safe and sound. Sit down now, and eat your breakfast."

Truman sat at the long trestle table, heaped grits on his plate, covered them with a hunk of fresh butter, and asked where I was. I'd been in the chicken house gathering more eggs. I put the eggs on the kitchen counter, washed my hands in the sink, and took my place at the table beside Truman. Even though it was only eight o'clock in the morning, we knew it was going to be another scorching day.

"I don't know what you boys have planned," Mother said, "but the wedding starts this afternoon at two. We need to be at the church by one-thirty in order to get seated."

Truman and I went on eating. Then Truman spoke. "Has Fred Jones still got any goats over there?"

"Got plenty. All sizes. He'll sell you one," Mother said.

Truman drank a big glass of fresh, cold milk. "After breakfast, let's pay Fred a visit."

"Okay," I said, thinking some barbecued goat would taste mighty good.

We took a roll of rope, borrowed Daddy's truck, and drove across the pasture to Fred Jones's house. "Well, if it ain't Masser Truman! How you been, sir?" Fred said, grinning from ear to ear.

"I'm fine, Fred. How are you and Bama doing?"

"We's gittin' along fine. Gittin' along some in age, but we's managing."

"Good," Truman said.

"What can I help y'all with today?" Fred asked. Then he winked. "Ain't gonna go dig up no more bones, is you?"

We had a good laugh, remembering the skeleton. "No, that's not why we're here. I want to buy one of your little nanny goats," Truman said.

"Well, come on over here to the fence with me," Fred said. We got out of the truck and followed Fred through the ankle-high grass to the edge of the fence. A flock of goats in all sizes grazed lazily. "Now big Billy, he ain't for sale. He's the daddy of 'em all. Without the big Billy, I wouldn't have no goats to eat or sell."

Truman spied a small goat, about three hands high. It was white with brown spots. "That one," he said.

"Sure is a scrawny little one," I said. "Ain't hardly enough on it to eat. Looks like she's still nursing."

"I want that one," Truman said.

Fred opened the fence, chased down the little goat, and grabbed it by its back feet. He took it to the truck where Truman and I roped the goat's feet together and laid the bleating little animal in the back of the truck. Truman gave Fred a dollar for the goat, to which Fred replied, "Thank you. That's plenty, Masser Truman." Then Truman and I drove back to my house with the wide-eyed goat bleating in fear as it bumped along on the floor of the old truck.

I parked the truck in the shade. "I've got to wash up and dress to be at the wedding on time," I said. "How about you?"

"You go ahead. I'll be there in a few minutes," said Truman.

I went on inside, thinking Truman would probably pen up the little goat in Mother's smokehouse, or tie it in the shade of the scuppernong arbor until late that afternoon, when we'd have to kill and dress it to barbecue. I didn't see Truman again before I left for the wedding with Mother and Daddy.

When we arrived at the church it was a particularly hot afternoon, sultry, without a breath of air stirring. People were arriving early for the wedding, for after all, when two young people from the town's high society married, it was a social event. The stained-glass windows were tilted open to let in some air. The organ music played. Sweet-smelling white lilies gave off a lingering scent mingled with the odors of beeswax candles. Bunches of waxy, green magnolia leaves draped down the windowsills. The church was filled to capacity. At least three hundred of the town's most prominent people were there. The music began. The soprano sang. I glanced anxiously about for Truman but still there was no sign of him. Mother punched me and said, "Quit looking back. You know it's unmannerly to look back in church. Truman'll be along when he gets good and ready. He's probably going to bring Jenny."

Finally it was time for the wedding march. Ham and his father entered the church and took their places to wait for the wedding procession. Bridesmaids streamed down the aisle in their pale yellow dresses. The congregation sang a hymn. Then the bride, radiant in a white dress with a long, flowing train, beamed as she walked down the aisle on her father's arm. Soft whispers of "Oh, isn't this the loveliest wedding Monroeville has ever seen?" floated through the air.

The guests took their seats and the minister began the ceremony. Everyone, including the bride, was sweltering. People in the congregation fanned themselves with paper church fans. The candles and some of the lilies began to droop. About this time a sound like a baby crying, *"Maaaa, Maaaa,"* filled the church. Everyone perked up and looked around. When the sound came again, even Ham and his bride turned around to see what was going on.

Then a deep, gravelly voice said, "I *knew* she had a baby. That's why she's having to marry him! That's her baby crying!"

The minister continued the ceremony and there was calm for a time, then *"Maaaa, Maaaa."* The bride's uncle excused himself, got up, and walked around to see who had brought a baby into the church.

Again, the gravelly voice said, "That's her baby crying. I knew she had to get married. Looks like she'd better go and tend to her baby."

About that time my ears perked up. I recognized the voice and knew what was going on. *Truman! You rascal. You've ruined Ham's wedding with that little goat!* I thought.

Then, thoughts of absolute stark terror hit: Mother knows Truman and I went after a goat this morning! What if she links me to Truman in this? Surely she recognizes his voice. Daddy'll kill me for sure if he thinks I helped Truman with this stunt. I broke out in a cold sweat.

Meanwhile, several of the bride's and groom's family members left the church and went outside to see where the sound was coming from. Inside, the wedding party and guests heard one loud *"Maaaaa!"* then the sound of *"Maaaa, Maaaa,"* fading in the distance as someone untied the bleating goat and led it away. When calm was restored, the minister heard some hurried "I do"s, then quickly pronounced the couple "man and wife." Then the bride and groom fled the church, literally running up the aisle.

I rode in the car to the reception with Mother and Daddy. Mother went on and on about "Where is Truman? What in the world was all that commotion about? Who on earth would want to spoil such a wonderful day for this lovely young couple? I just don't understand where Truman is."

Hundreds of guests gathered at the bride's home for what was to have been the most elegant bridal reception in Monroeville. While we stood in line sipping pineapple punch from a dainty glass cup and waited on the bride and groom, Mother turned to me. "Have you seen Truman, Jennings Faulk? Do you know where he is? If we're going to have barbecued goat for supper, somebody better get on home. It takes awhile to get the fire going in the pit, and it'll take several hours to clean and cook that goat."

I doubted we would have any barbecued goat for supper, but I didn't say a word. Like everyone else at the reception, I drank punch, ate wedding cake, and waited for a bride and groom who never showed up.

When we got back to our house late that afternoon, Mother went off looking for Truman and the goat, but neither could be found. Daddy changed out of his one good suit and back into work clothes and went to feed the cows. Truman had packed his bags and left, which was very unlike him. He always had long good-byes with hugs and promises to come back soon, to write, and keep in touch. But not this time. I thought it was rude that he just up and left. But considering the way he'd acted since he hit town, ruining Ham's wedding, I wasn't surprised. I couldn't believe he'd pulled this stunt with the goat and gotten away with it. I guess he thought nobody would find out. But I knew. And it showed me that the "old" Truman I'd known was changing. The little-boy vindictiveness had taken an adult form. He was, as Sook had said, "grown now."

# Epilogue

*I'm not a saint yet.*
*I'm an alcoholic.*
*I'm a drug addict.*
*I'm homosexual.*
*I'm a genius.*

TRUMAN CAPOTE, "Nocturnal Turnings"

*W*e always looked on Truman as being different. We thought he had turned his back on the family in Monroeville, and he did; but in retrospect, I can see why. I really think he had good reasons. Frankly, I'm surprised he was as patient with us as he was, because each of us failed him in our own way.

The Faulks are notoriously indifferent to other people's problems or success. It's their own little immediate world that's important to them and has great priority. Truman's mother, Lillie Mae, for instance, was so wrapped up in her own interests that he rarely saw her. Whenever he turned to her for comfort and approval, I suspect she was so involved in trying to be a socialite and nursing her wounds as a frustrated actress that Truman was unable to break through to her. When she later turned to drugs and alcohol, she was unavailable to him emotionally. I don't think Truman ever forgave her for burning up his notebooks and all the stories he'd kept since childhood. He got back at her, though, because when she died he had her cremated, knowing she was afraid of fire.

He had great affection for my mother, Mary Ida, and shifted his "mother instincts" to her early in his life. The two sisters looked a little bit alike. They both certainly had the Faulk personality, except that Mother was a devoted wife and mother. But Mother was so wrapped up in her world that Truman was somewhat of an outsider. She was all he had, however, after Lillie Mae and Sook died. So he came to see her often, wrote letters, and called her.

One time when Truman came to see us he was driving Joe Capote's car. Most of the times he came from New York it was with Joe and Lillie Mae, but this time they were off on a trip to Bermuda, and he'd struck out on his own. It was 1948, right after he'd sold *Other Voices, Other Rooms.* When he arrived that day, he was so proud! After years of writing and striving for success, he'd finally sold a book. He wanted the family to be proud of him and share this happy time. Beaming all over, he tried to keep the conversation on his writing.

But instead of Mother saying "Congratulations!" and giving him a pat on the back, she turned her usual indifferent shoulder to him. She glossed over his success, turning the conversation to questions about Lillie Mae and Joe. "Where are they? Why aren't you with them? When are they coming to Monroeville?" I could tell that Truman's feelings were hurt. Not one to show it, he put on a stiff upper lip and said, "I'm on a business trip to New Orleans to see about some writing, and that's why I'm here. I decided to stop by for a short visit."

Truman's great comfort and love in his youth was Sook.

He was smart enough to recognize that even though she was a great "pretend" companion and mental-age playmate, she was not a mother image who could guide him. Even though Sook was all good and wouldn't have steered anyone in the wrong direction, she didn't have the capacity to be a mother to him. So he failed in trying to find a mother image there. Truman searched for a father about as desperately as he looked for a mother. But he failed all the way around. Joe Capote did everything to try to capture Truman's affection. Perhaps he tried *too hard* with money, private schools, and lavish gifts rather than with personal attention, because Truman never did feel close to Joe.

After Truman became a financial success in the 1950s, his natural father, Arch Persons, suddenly remembered that Truman was his son. He went to great pains to cultivate Truman. He entertained him and visited him, but again, Truman's long memory kept him barely speaking to Arch.

Then there was my father. He failed Truman as well. After Truman became famous, he still had not forgotten Monroeville. There was a thirty-acre farm that joined my daddy's land at the creek. A little wood-frame farmhouse stood in the creek bottom at Hatter's Mill, where Truman had saved Edison McMillan's life the day Edison tried to steam down the mill. Truman remembered the house from the time he was a boy and had long been infatuated with it. He thought perhaps he'd buy it, squirrel up in there, shut the gate, and use it as a writer's retreat. Mother would be only a mile away, so he could walk across the field and be with her if he wanted a cup of coffee and someone to talk to.

A friend of Daddy's lived out there on the property. Truman asked Daddy if he would speak to Ben Jones, the owner, and get him to sell. The price wasn't unreasonable. Ben agreed to sell and the deal was about to be consummated when Daddy got to thinking about the situation. He told Ben, "Better not sell that land to Truman because all these strange, weird writers, musicians, and dope addicts will be out there running through the woods, tearing down the fences, and letting the cows out. There won't be a moment's peace. Somebody'll always be coming over to see Mary Ida and me and worrying us, and this'll interrupt our entire life. I think it'll be better for us if you don't sell." So Truman didn't get his country retreat.

Even his teachers and friends fell short. I remember when Truman started to school in Monroeville, the one thing he was really proud of and should have been recognized for was his absolute genius with words. He had an enormous vocabulary, was an excellent speller, and had learned to read and write before he ever started school. He thought this would make him important to his teacher and the other students. Instead, the teacher resented him knowing so much, because he was so far superior to the other children in the class. The children turned on him because he was different. They made life hard by picking on him.

The only true friend he had that wasn't family was Nelle Harper Lee. When they were children, Nelle would comfort him and say, "It's all right, Truman, that you know everything, even if the teachers don't understand." Later Nelle failed him, too. She was the sweetheart image in his young life, but for whatever reasons, at a time when he wanted a sweetheart and lover, she could not be this.

Probably the greatest insult Truman had to take from any of us was the time he brought his male lover to Mother and Daddy's house. Truman was acting very much like a young bride, all flushed and happy. He arrived one summer for Mother and Daddy to appraise his friend and see what they thought about the situation. Truman parked the Jaguar under the trees, and they came into the house. When it finally dawned on Mother and Daddy what the relationship was between the two men, Daddy laughed, but Mother had one of her cursing, screaming fits. She literally ran the man out of the house and chased him into the car. She forbade him to set foot in her house again. Truman was crestfallen. He hung his head and didn't say anything as he followed his friend out of the house and drove away. From then on, when Truman came to visit, he was alone.

I was another of the relatives who failed him. When World War II began, I was consumed with patriotism. The war dominated my every thought. I ridiculed Truman for not wanting to take part, for not wanting to be a good soldier. That's all I could see then. The very last thing he wanted to be was a soldier. He had never wanted any part of fighting, even as a child, but I didn't understand him nor did I want to.

Other family members, like Mother's brother, Seabon, ridiculed Truman by making fun of his homosexuality and snickering behind Truman's back. Then when Truman began doing well financially, Seabon's attitude swung completely around. He went so far as to go and live with Truman as a "handyman" at one time.

I think Truman finally reached a point in life where he thought everybody wanted a piece of him. One day after he had become famous and wealthy, he was sitting on the front porch talking with Mother, Daddy, and me. Mother said, "Now that you've written the ultimate book, *In Cold Blood*, what are you going to write next?"

Out of the blue Truman said, "To tell you the truth, I might not ever write another line." Mother jumped up and said, "But Truman! What about all those contracts you signed! What about all that money you took to write that other book!"

He just laughed and said, "I've already written the world's best short story, 'A Christmas Memory,' and I've written one of the world's best books, *In Cold Blood.* They can wipe their behinds with those contracts, because now I've got plenty of money!"

Truman's final insult was the curtain call of his life, for he only lived about a year after that. He had boarded an airplane to come and visit Mother. But by the time he arrived in Montgomery, he was so ill he had to be taken directly to the hospital. He called Mother again and again. Even the doctors called. Mother tried explaining to Truman that she was in bad health and a four-hour round trip to see him would be very hard on her. Her brother-in-law, Marvin Carter, was in the same hospital having surgery, but he couldn't have company. Mother told Truman she would visit him when she could see Marvin, too.

When we arrived at the hospital several days later, Truman had checked out. Mother's face fell in disappointment. We never saw Truman again. We had all failed him one last time. When we next heard about Truman, he was dead. That was August 24, 1984. He died in a house in California, a state he hated, without any family around him.

Perhaps he knew his would be such an end when he penned these words in the story "Nocturnal Turnings":

*TC: Let's say our old prayer. The one we used to say when we were little and slept in the same bed with Sook and Queenie, with the quilts piled on top of us because the house was so big and cold.*
*TC: Our old prayer? Okay.*
*TC and TC: Now I lay me down to sleep, I pray the Lord my soul to*

*keep. And if I should die before I wake, I pray the Lord my soul to take.
Amen.*
TC: *Goodnight.*
TC: *Goodnight.*
TC: *I love you.*
TC: *I love. you, too.*
TC: *You'd better. Because when you get right down to it, all we've got is
each other. Alone. To the grave. And that's the tragedy, isn't it?*
TC: *You forget. We have God, too.*
TC: *Yes. We have God.*
TC: *Zzzzzzz*
TC: *Zzzzzzzz*
TC and TC: *Zzzzzzzzz*

# INDEX

Capote, Joseph (*cont'd*)
  described, 27, 165
  embezzlement by, 184˙
  at Orange Beach, 65–72
  Truman and, 32–33, 165,
    214–15, 226
Capote, Lillie Mae Faulk, 40,
    101, 182, 203, 225
  abandonment of Capote, 19,
    26–27, 32, 45, 81, 164
  as an alcoholic, 214, 215,
    218, 224
  birth of, 23
  burned notebooks and, 214–
    15, 224
  "calling" on neighbors and,
    118
  death of, 224
  described, 66, 67
  Jenny and, 24–27, 107
  marriage of, 25–27
  at Orange Beach, 65–72
  remarriage of, 27, 51
  tricycle airplane and, 98–
    100
Capote, Truman
  abandoned to the care of rel-
    atives, 19, 26–39, 45, 80–
    82, 164
  addiction to tranquilizers, 17–
    18
  advice about writing, 12–13
  as an adult, 10–18, 214–23
  alcoholism of, 16, 17–18

autobiographical works of, 6,
    19, 116
Big Boy and, 5, 6, 15, 16, 18,
    28, 34–41
birth of, 26
Boss and, 142, 146–49
as "Broadway talent scout,"
    204–13
"calling" on neighbors and,
    118
Captain Wash and, 73–82
as character in *To Kill a Mock-
    ingbird,* 6, 33, 64
childhood of, 33–40, 173
cotton-bale caper and, 173–
    85
country retreat of, 226–27
cowardice of, 204, 212
crying, 106, 181–82
in Cuba, 203, 204, 208
death of, 229
described, 11, 17–18, 74,
    150–51, 173, 203–204, 215
the draft and, 40, 214
as an eccentric, 5, 16, 39, 224
epilogue, 224–30
fame and fortune of, 15, 17,
    184, 228–29
farm life and, 35–36, 150–51,
    164–65
father of. *See* Persons, Arch
fear of physical pain, 204
fighting and, 147–49, 204,
    228